UNCERTAIN TRUMPET

Uncertain Trumpet

THE PRIEST IN MODERN AMERICA

by ANDREW M. GREELEY

SHEED AND WARD: NEW YORK

© *Sheed and Ward, Inc., 1968*

Library of Congress Catalog Card Number 68–13841

Nihil Obstat:
  Leo J. Steady
  Censor Librorum

Imprimatur:
  †Robert F. Joyce
  Bishop of Burlington
  October 3, 1967

The Nihil Obstat and Imprimatur are official declarations that a book or pamphlet is considered to be free of doctrinal or moral error. No implication is contained herein that those who have granted the Nihil Obstat or the Imprimatur agree with the contents, opinions or statements expressed.

Manufactured in the United States of America

For the Durkins—
  Jack
  Mary Jule
  Mary Laura
  Julie
  Eileen
  Sean
  Danny
  Ann
  Elizabeth . . .

Contents

vii

Introduction

I SHALL RESIST all temptations to apologize for presenting these ideas for priestly reflection. In the Church after the Vatican Council it would be unworthy of a priest to apologize for offering points for consideration and discussion to fellow members of the presbyterate. I do not expect agreement with my notions, and they are not presented with the intention of demanding agreement. He who agrees with my thoughts does me honor; but he who uses my thoughts as an occasion for developing his own thoughts does me much greater honor. I will not pretend in these pages to a style of piety I do not have, nor will I express regrets over the extensive use of sociological and psychological categories in these chapters. It is my conviction that the social sciences have much to tell us about piety, both Christian and priestly, and I do not propose to modify this conviction because others do not share it.

AG

Who is the happy warrior? Who is he
That every man in arms should wish to be?
It is the Generous Spirit, who, when brought
Among the tasks of real life, hath wrought
Upon the plan that pleased his childish thought;
Whose high endeavours are an inward light
That makes the path before him always bright:
Who with a natural instinct to discern
What knowledge can perform, is diligent to learn.

—Wordsworth, "The Happy Warrior"

UNCERTAIN TRUMPET

1

The Modern World and the Priest

ANYONE WHO TRIES to evaluate the work of the priest in the modern world must take as his basic starting point the premise that the Catholic Church is going through profound, drastic, and intensely painful change, perhaps the most dramatic change since Paul persuaded Peter that Gentile converts should not be held by Jewish law, and the Church cut itself off from the synagogue. The crisis of change we are going through now is not just a minor readjustment. It is not a small modification of the existing status quo. It is not the introduction of a certain limited number of novelties in Church activities. It is, in fact, a revolution and the abandonment of a style and posture that for all practical purposes was established at the Council of Trent and has persisted in the Church for four centuries. Those of us who are over thirty have served our priestly lives both in the counterreformation and post-ecumenical Church and, unless we have the courage and the strength to face the staggering implications of the change between two eras that occurred in the midst of our lives, we will find ourselves inevitably drifting farther and farther away from the mainstream of the life of the Church. In a very few years we will become merely curious relics of a bygone era.

We may, if it be our pleasure, view the old Church as superior to the new Church, though such a view would imply that the Holy Spirit somehow or other stopped working when John XXIII convened the Second Vatican Council. But if we persist in lamenting for the glories of the past instead of facing the pains and uncertainties and opportunities of the present, we will find that our lives and our ministry will become as pertinent to the problems of our people as the comfortable political theories of the 1890's are relevant to the political realities the United States faces in the 1960's.

We may seek comfort in the contention that nothing basic in priestly life can ever change, that people's problems are the same as they ever were, and that the fundamental elements in the priestly ministry need not change. But, if such is the nature of our style at the present moment, then we become like the ostrich who is afraid to take his head out of the sand and the dinosaur who, for all his great bulk, was simply unable to adapt to change. We may reassure ourselves, but we will not persuade anyone, for all our self-satisfaction, that we are in fact right; we will fail our people and we will fail in our vocation. The priest who refuses to acknowledge that the world is changing drastically, that the Church is changing drastically, and that the priesthood must change drastically is a priest who has lost his nerve. A priest without courage and nerve is a useless priest.

Yet, we were able as priests to isolate ourselves from the rapidly moving currents of contemporary life more effectively than almost any other professionals at work in the world. The bonds of loyalty (frequently the result of the ethnic immigrant group experience) which have held together our parishes are primordial and powerful and, hence, we could successfully ignore most of the changes in the world around us.

As long as people flocked to church on Sunday, we had no concern about the impact of TV on parish organizations and religious devotion. As long as the young people loyally came to confession, we did not have to worry about the effect of the automobile on teen-age morality. As long as the most successful and enlightened of our lay people were docilely obedient to us, we did not have to worry about the effect of higher education on the attitude of our laity. As long as there were enough curates to meet our immediate needs, we did not have to be concerned about the implication of the sudden decline in vocations, though we did lament that it did make our school budgets much higher than we would have liked. As long as one Catholic family moving out was replaced by another Catholic family moving in, the incredible geographic mobility of the jet age was not so terribly important to us. As long as young priests did what they were told, the implications of the psychological age on the attitude of curates was not a matter of great moment to us. And, as long as there was no thought of liturgical change in the United States, we did not have to worry about the results of worldwide travel on an increasing proportion of our people. No matter what kind of odd liturgy they saw in France or Germany or Belgium or Holland, we could assure them that that sort of thing would never happen in the United States. The traditional ethnic parish of the early and middle twentieth century seemed quite secure from change and from being notably affected by the dynamic progress of the world beyond it.

As priests, we probably could have remained indifferent to the changing modern world if the Church itself had not begun to read the signs of the times. But now that the Church has indeed turned to the signs of the times, we too must heed these signs if we are to be loyal sons of the Church. As we begin to read them, we understand how tenuous was the protective security of the parish life and how our efforts in the parish are becoming more and more irrelevant to the real religious problems of our people. We must, therefore, force ourselves to be open to the signs of the times, to interpret them, to find their meaning, and then to apply their meaning, as the Church does, to our lives and work.

In this respect, the Pastoral Constitution on the Church in the Modern World must become almost a bible for the priest. He must read it, and reread it, and reread it once again to see that his own vision and his own work are as broad and as profound as that of the Church which he claims to serve. Particularly must he read paragraphs four through ten of the Pastoral Constitution, for here in the clearest possible words the Church describes the problems of the modern world, pronounces its sympathy with those seeking solution to the problems, and urges all members of the Church, and one would presume especially the clergy, to be aware of the implication of the times for their own lives. At least some passages must be quoted explicitly:*

Today, the human race is passing through a new stage of its history. Profound and rapid changes are spreading by degrees around the whole world. Triggered by the intelligence and

---

* Excerpts from the Constitutions and Decrees of the Ecumenical Council are taken from *The Documents of Vatican II*, published by Guild Press, America Press, Association Press, and Herder and Herder, and copyrighted 1966 by The America Press. Used by permission.

creative energies of man, these changes recoil upon him, upon his decisions and desires, both individual and collective, and upon his manner of thinking and acting with respect to things and to people. Hence we can already speak of a true social and cultural transformation, one which has repercussions on man's religious life as well. (202)

As happens in any crisis of growth, this transformation has brought serious difficulties in its wake. Thus while man extends his power in every direction, he does not always succeed in subjecting it to his own welfare. Striving to penetrate farther into the deeper recesses of his own mind, he frequently appears more unsure of himself. Gradually and more precisely he lays bare the laws of society, only to be paralyzed by uncertainty about the direction to give it. (202)

Advances in biology, psychology, and the social sciences not only bring men hope of improved self-knowledge. In conjunction with tecnical methods, they are also helping men to exert direct influence on the life of social groups. At the same time, the human race is giving ever-increasing thought to forecasting and regulating its own population growth. (203)

New and more efficient media of social communication are contributing to the knowledge of events. By setting off chain reactions, they are giving the swiftest and widest possible circulation to styles of thought and feeling. (204)

A change in attitudes and in human structures frequently calls accepted values into question. This is especially true of young people, who have grown impatient on more than one occasion, and indeed become rebels in their distress. Aware of their own influence in the life of society, they want to assume a role in it sooner. As a result, parents and educators frequently experience greater difficulties day by day in discharging their tasks. (205)

The institutions, laws, and modes of thinking and feeling as handed down from previous generations do not always seem to be well adapted to the contemporary state of affairs. Hence arises an upheaval in the manner and even the norms of behavior. (205)

Finally, these new conditions have their impact on religion. On the one hand a more critical ability to distinguish religion from a magical view of the world and from the superstitions which still circulate purifies religion and exacts day by day a more personal and explicit adherence to faith. As a result many persons are achieving a more vivid sense of God. (205)

On the other hand, growing numbers of people are abandoning religion in practice. Unlike former days, the denial of God or of religion, or the abandonment of them, are no longer unusual and individual occurrences. For today it is not rare for such decisions to be presented as requirements of scientific progress or of a certain new humanism. In numerous places these views are voiced not only in the teachings of philosophers, but on every side they influence literature, the arts, the interpretation of the humanities and of history, and civil laws themselves. As a consequence, many people are shaken. (205)

Meanwhile, the conviction grows not only that humanity can and should increasingly consolidate its control over creation, but even more, that it devolves on humanity to establish a

political, social, and economic order which will to an even
better extent serve man and help individuals as well as groups
to affirm and develop the dignity proper to them. (206)

The tragedy of our training and our lives is that we
know so little about these signs of the times and find it so
difficult to interpret their implications for our own life
and work. We are often afraid even to begin to think
about these questions, and dismiss those who raise them
as dreamers or visionaries who know nothing of the practical problems of the parish. The harsh truth is that if we
do not listen to the dreamers and visionaries who raise
these questions (that is to say, the Fathers of the Vatican
Council), then before very long we will find that we have
no parishes, because no one who persists on living in the
past can expect over the long run to influence those who
live in the present. Nor can those who look to the past
as a golden age expect to have any impact at all on those
confidently planning for a better future.

The problems of the transition of the Church from a
post-Tridentine to a post-Vatican age are reinforced in
our country by the fact that the American Catholic population has finally come abreast socially, economically,
and politically of the Protestant population. We are no
longer immigrants, and in a few years we will no longer
even have many of the children of the immigrants among
our numbers. We are as well educated and as successful

in business and professions as any other Americans. The priest who still views the Catholic population as relatively uneducated, naive, simple working folk, docilely obedient to their priests and their Church, is engaging in self-deception. The pastor who proudly told a visitor that the core of his parish were the "cap and sweater" people is living in the past and refusing to realize the traditional Catholic parish, organized to deal with the problems of the ethnic immigrant community, must be drastically overhauled if it is to be any help at all in an age when most of its members are the grandchildren of the immigrants.

The result of the interaction of these two transitions from slum to suburb and from counterreformation to ecumenical Church is a time of great anxiety, confusion, and ambiguity. It is a time of profound reexamination, of the stripping away of those accidental characteristics of the priestly ministry that are no longer relevant. It is a time of careful examination, and reexamination, evaluation and reevaluation. The excess baggage from the outmoded past must be resolutely discarded if it is an obstacle or a hindrance to the work of the present moment. We must come to realize, for example, that invitations which say monsignors vest in the rectory and priests vest in the school hall do not in fact represent an immutable order of nature. We must come to understand that the essentials of the priesthood are clearly stated by the Vatican Council: the priests must build up the people of God by preaching the word of God, presiding over the Eucharistic assembly, and leading them through service in charity. Those elements in clerical culture which impede, or which do not contribute notably to, the achievement of these goals must go as quickly as possible.

The reevaluation and reexamination which are part of renewal take courage, flexibility, and hope, precisely those virtues which our training and our experience have often failed to develop in us. Transitions are ambiguous, uncertain, and painful, and those of us who are not mature enough to cope with such ambiguity can readily choose one of two extremes. We can, on the one hand, refuse to consider the signs of the times, refuse to admit the facts of change, refuse to admit the need for drastic reform and renewal in our ministry, refuse to acknowledge the need for drastic reconsideration of what the priesthood ought to mean. We can refuse even to read books about the Vatican Council for fear such volumes will disturb our peace and serenity, or we can, on the other hand, conclude that everything out of the past must be discarded on *a priori* grounds, that reevaluation and reconsideration to separate what is good in the tradition from what is no longer relevant is a waste of time because there is virtually nothing in the tradition that can be any help to us in the present.

The first is the mistake of the old breed and the second

is the mistake of the new breed, and both of these reactions have a common element: their immaturity, their refusal to go through the painful process of reevaluation which means that some things will have their value reinforced and others will be revealed as having little value. The immaturity of both the old breed and the new breed demonstrates a lack of nerve and steadiness, a lack of growth, an inability to cope with uncertainty and ambiguity, a fear of facing hard questions in a time when hard questions must be asked, an abdication of responsibility and leadership. It is difficult to say whether the extremes of the old breed or the extremes of the new breed are worse, but unless the majority of priests refuse to accept either form of extremism, the Catholic Church of the United States is in bad trouble.

One can readily judge the years in which we will exercise our priesthood as a time of great frustration, nervousness, anxiety, and distraction. One can, I think with equal realism, also judge that ours is a time of great joy and excitement and challenge. We are going through the most critical time since the Church first hesitantly poked its head out of the walls of Jerusalem; we are going through a time when the Church will reshape itself in a fashion that will affect perhaps the next millennium. For years to come men will look back on our age and envy us for the privilege of living during such great and stirring times. The priest of the future will find it very difficult to believe

that there could have lived in our day priests who were
afraid of the opportunities of the present moment. The
critical question then for us is whether we have the nerve,
the open-mindedness, the hardheadedness, and the class
to carry it off.

2

The Quest
for Maturity

A PRIEST I KNOW tells a story of two pastors with whom he worked. The first was a terribly anxious, nervous man who found decisions extremely difficult to make. Unfortunately, his parish school was located across the parking lot from the rectory. Some of the adolescent members of the parish, as teen-agers are wont to do, were occasionally given to deliberately or indeliberately throwing various objects through the school windows. When the pastor would look from his vantage point in the rectory across the parking lot and see the shattered windows, he would be overwhelmed by anxiety and depression. Another window had been broken, and what was he to do about it? He could not even muster the emotional vigor to instruct the janitor to replace the shattered glass. My informant, dreading the days of tension and anxiety around the rectory produced by each new smashed window, managed to obtain a fairly large supply of plate glass and instructed the janitor to replace broken windows early in the morning before the pastor could come upon them. By this stroke of diplomatic genius the curate greatly eased the anxiety in the rectory.

Alas, the pastor finally despaired of ever solving his problems and resigned. His successor arrived, made a hasty inspection of the parish plant, and severely reprimanded the hapless assistant for having such an oversupply of plate glass on hand. He was an efficient administrator and would tolerate no explanation of why such an uneconomic and inefficient stockpile of glass would be required. As the curate remarked, "No matter what you try, you are bound to lose."

The point of the story is that both pastors in question behaved immaturely (and let me emphasize here that assistants, in their own fashion, and residents and every other kind and variety of priests are as capable of immature behavior as pastors). The first could not make a decision no matter how much data he had available, and the second felt that no data was necessary before he could make his decisions. Such orientations might be harmless in another age, but in an era of ambiguity and uncertainty immaturity is disastrous.

What are the marks of the mature man?

1. He is able to make decisions and live with them. He is bothered neither by a compulsiveness which forces him to premature decisions, nor by an insecurity which prevents him from making decisions when they ought to be made, nor, finally, by guilt feelings which necessitate hours of self-torment once the decision has been made.

2. He is able to tolerate a high level of ambiguity and uncertainty in his life, and it does not matter whether the ambiguity and uncertainty flow from some other's decisions or his own. He is secure enough in his own selfhood not to be overwhelmed by the fluidity of the world around him.

3. He is able to relate in an intelligent and open way with superiors and subordinates. He is not overawed by the power and majesty of those above him nor terrified by the secretiveness and independence of those beneath him. He does not fawn over his superiors nor dominate his inferiors. He is able to be independent of those in authority and also to generate independence and initiative in those under his authority. He welcomes criticisms from above and below but does not necessarily accept the former as dogma nor the latter as necessary idiocies. The basic humanity which he shares with his superiors and his subordinates is far more important to him than the accidents of rank or distinction.

4. He is able to recognize his own emotional problems and live with them in some kind of peace until he can

eliminate them, and he has no need to deceive himself about the origins of these problems. He does not project the cause of his internal anxieties into the world outside him. He does not blame the seminary, or the parish to which he is assigned, or his pastor, or his lay people, or his assistants, or his bishop, or Negroes, or anyone else for insecurities and uncertainties which he knows are inside himself.

5. He is able to give himself in full human relationships without any fear that others will trample upon him or that he will be swept away by the power of his emotions. He, therefore, finds no need to hide behind the defense mechanisms of erratic and idiosyncratic behavior or caste distinctions which clergy so successfully use to keep the lay people at an antiseptic distance from themselves.

6. He respects and loves himself. He realizes that self-hatred, at least of the neurotic variety, is not humility but, in fact, pride. He respects his own dignity and his own value, his own worth, his own goodness. He knows that there are vast areas for improvement in his personality, but he does not so reject himself that he becomes a mere pawn moved about by the wind of external pressures outside his personality.

7. He is in possession of himself. There is in his personality a hard inner core of selfhood which does not merely react or respond to the outside world but takes charge of the self in the world. His personality is not a

series of masks, not a collection of frightened reactions, not an amorphous blob of behavioral variables rocked about on a current of confusion and uncertainty. On the contrary, because he accepts himself and loves himself, because he is able to affirm his own worth and goodness, he is able to take charge of himself; he possesses what the psychologists call ego-strength. He has accepted his own destiny, affirmed that destiny, and now is in control of the direction which the destiny has taken.

8. He respects others because he respects himself. Thus, those outside his own personality are not external threats to his selfhood but real selves just like himself, capable of loving and feeling and hurting, and needing love and respect and affirmation of value. Only because he respects himself is he able to respect others, and only because he respects others is he able to give himself to others in a mature and loving relationship.

The major problem in our lives as priests, however we may subscribe in theory to the excellence of this picture of maturity I have presented, is that our training in the seminary and our experiences in the rectory environment have conspired to prevent most of us, and here I surely include myself, from achieving the degree of maturity that seems to be essential for us to survive the confusion, the complexities, and the ambiguities of the present moment. We are, therefore, faced with the painful necessity

of maturing, and maturing rapidly, or simply being overwhelmed by the chaos we see around us. Growing up
humanly is never an easy task and becomes much more
difficult when we have to start it in the late thirties or the
forties or the fifties.

I might note in passing that while the language of emotional maturity I have used tends to be the language of
the new breed, it does not therefore follow that the new
breed of priests are more likely to practice it than anyone
else. A member of the new breed must demonstrate that
he is capable of learning from the wisdom of the past, of
respecting others in the context in which they have found
themselves. Only when he has proved that he does not
confuse external superficialities with critical problems will
I be persuaded that a member of the new breed has any
more claim than anyone else to the virtue of emotional
maturity. When a member of the new breed shows up at
a party, at which all the laymen are wearing suits and
ties, clad in a sweater because he is ashamed to wear his
Roman collar, when he thinks he must be an expert teeny-
bopper to be human, when he thinks that it is part of the
humanism of the priesthood to frequent bars and night
clubs, when he is compelled to shock pious laity whenever possible and to make an exhibition of his own emotional difficulties to sophisticated laity whenever the opportunity arises, I am hardly prepared to concede that
this particular member of the new breed is mature.

I trust that it is not necessary for me to affirm that this somewhat sarcastic description is not aimed at all young priests, or even the majority of them, or even a substantial minority of them, but I want to emphasize that the ability to make sophisticated use of the language of emotional maturity does not guarantee that the user himself has achieved that maturity.

The basic problem for all of us, and again I shall include myself near the top of the list, is that our training and experience were aimed, and perhaps not indeliberately, at keeping us immature, which was taken to mean the same thing as docile and obedient. It would be less than realistic to deny that the training was successful. Those who supervised us both in the seminary and after ordination feared strong men, men who knew who they were and what their priesthood was and who would not permit, under any circumstances, their basic human dignity to be violated. Strong men such as these develop only when there are freedom, the opportunity for initiative and responsibility, the chance for decision-making, and a respect for the uniqueness, the security, and the dignity of the individual human personality. We were trained, and have been treated through most of our lives, as priests in a way that made it extraordinarily difficult to develop self-respect. We had to suppress so much, pretend so often, simulate so frequently, that deep down inside, most of us, I fear, had every reason to suspect that we were phonies. Under such circumstances, it is quite impossible to relate to anyone else, be it a fellow priest, a superior, a subject, a lay person, a child in grammar school, in any kind of authentically human way. Eugene Kennedy, M.M., has suggested, for example, that one of the reasons so many priests, despite excellent training, are not good as counselors is that when the counseling situation becomes a relationship with all the human exchange that relationship implies, the priest becomes frightened and fears that he will lose himself in the relationship. Because of his lack of confidence and self-respect, he finds one way or another to discourage the client from returning for further counseling.

To put the matter more bluntly and more painfully, if we are trained in immaturity, or if we are deprived of opportunity for self-respect, then it is extraordinarily difficult for us to be able to love. If you do not love yourself, you cannot love others. And if you do not love, then challenge and vision are simply not part of your life. You are not able to cope with the rigorous implications of seeing things as they are, and also as they should be. So the results, therefore, are immaturity and mediocrity based ultimately on fear—fear especially of the inadequacies of the self. Fortunately, society provides us with a mask, a role, behind which we can hide our feeling of worthlessness. We can protect ourselves behind the Roman collar and behind the clericalist style of behavior. Beneath the front of the nice-guy priest, of the radical priest reformer, of the sociologist priest, or of the pious priest, there is often a disorganized, stunted, irresponsible, adolescent personality.

The adolescent priest is much less than human and seeks outlets for his own frustrations in a variety of foolishnesses, not excluding the turning of ecclesiastical and pastoral administration into the be-all and the end-all of the ministry. The ecclesiastical fund raiser, builder, bookkeeper, and caretaker, who is that and nothing else, has simply found a comfortable mask to hide his own feelings of emptiness and nothingness. And I could say the same thing for the flaming, alienated, young radical who hates the middle class, hates white people, hates the ecclesiastical structure, hates older priests, and, indeed, most powerfully hates himself. Obviously, I am not rejecting either administrative or radical reform as appropriate vehicles for priestly activity. They both represent the kinds of work that one supposes some priests should and must do, but when this kind of work becomes one's personality, then he is simply hiding his own immaturity and alienation.

The immature priest is exactly what is not required in the American Church at the present time. Some of us have made it to maturity in one fashion or another. For genetic or environmental reasons we developed enough ego-strength to become reasonably mature, full-fledged human beings. Some of us have made it part of the way. We really are not adults yet (of course, most people aren't adults either), but we do have the sense that we are growing and have the capacity for further growth. Others of us have the potential of making it if we put our minds to it, but our posture presently is one of immobility. We could grow, we may grow, but we are not, in fact, growing. Still others of us, it is to be feared, remain adolescents all our lives. Neither the pastorate nor the purple will get rid of our juvenile behavior and our adolescent defense mechanisms. We do not even have the strength of character and personality to admit that we have emotional problems, that our maturity is at least, to some extent, impeded. For the second and third group, and that I suppose includes most of us, it is important to emphasize that it is never too late to grow, that, no matter how old one is, he can still learn, can still come to understand himself, his problems and, at least in some fashion, to take possession of his own personality and direct it. It is possible, really no matter how old we are, to become the captain of our own ship and resist the forces and furies that swirl around us.

While I certainly would not want to go so far as to suggest counseling and psychotherapy for every priest, I do not doubt that many more of us would benefit by a fairly extensive counseling relationship than are willing to admit it. The crucial question is whether we are able to honestly recognize and face our fears and our insecurities and our silly defenses and our childish rivalries, to begin to make progress against them, begin indeed to emerge as an adult male. If we can say with some confidence that we are doing this, and doing it at something better than a snail's pace, then obviously we do not need outside help, though perhaps we could profit from it. But if we are bogged down and are not growing, then the sensible, intelligent, mature thing to do is seek help where it can best be found. It is a terribly hard thing for any presumed adult male to admit he cannot solve his problems by himself. It can be especially difficult for a priest to admit this. But to be able to admit it is the beginning of maturity and the beginning of becoming the kind of a priest that is absolutely essential in the confused, ambiguous world in which we must live and work.

3

Priest, Leader, and Teacher of the Christian Community

LAST YEAR I SPENT most of my time doing a study, for the Carnegie Corporation, of Catholic higher education. While I would hesitate to make specific comments about most of the thirty-six colleges and universities we visited, I have no hesitation at all in saying that the most warmly Christian institution we visited was Immaculate Heart College in Los Angeles. One of my more cynical colleagues on the staff of the project said to me after we had been in this truly unique institution for about two hours, "You know, there is something wrong with this place," to which I replied, "I feel it too, but I can't figure out what it is." And he responded, "All of these people are laughing."

Immaculate Heart College was a school filled with joy

and laughter. The sisters, the lay people, the administrators, the faculty, and the girls themselves were the hap-
piest group of human beings I have ever encountered in
my life. When, as a good sociologist must, I tried to find
an explanation for this unique institution, I was constantly referred to Mother Eucharia who had been the
Mother General of the Order and was now the principal
of the nearby high school. So I hied myself down to the
high school to interview this splendid lady. She offered
two explanations for the uniqueness of Immaculate Heart,
only one of which is relevant in the present context.

We feel in our Order the young woman who joins us is entrusted to us by God so that she might develop that which is
most completely and uniquely herself. It is not our task to
mold her or to form her, to direct her down any preconceived
lines. We rather try to create a climate where she is as free
as she possibly can be to develop that which is best in her
own talents and personality. We feel that the talents God
has given a young woman are an indication of what he wants
her to do and what he wants her to become, and it would be
almost blasphemous on our part to interfere with God's will
which is so clearly manifest in the talents and inclinations he
has given her. Our religious order exists simply to facilitate
the development of that which is best in all of those who come
to us.

Mother Eucharia's very powerful and moving description of the role of the Sisters of the Immaculate Heart is

a marvelous description of the role of the priest in the Church. Bishop Remi De Roo of Canada, one of the more sophisticated theologians of the Vatican Council, has pointed out to me that one of the powerful new or renewed insights at the Council was that the priest, as leader of the Christian community, must not only recognize but do everything in his power to encourage the charisma of the various members of the community. Indeed, it is primarily by serving his people in such a way that they are encouraged to develop their own talents and charisms that the priest contributes to the upbuilding of the Christian community. As Bishop Young has said with reference to the Conciliar document on the priesthood:

To form a community, with a deep sense of its own identity, not static and hidebound by a constricting parochialism, but open in love and action to the wider community of the whole Church and the world—this is the challenge the Council throws down to her priests. To train men and women to Christian maturity that will flow over into free, loving action in the community of their fellowmen, and to recognize the gifts and insights freely dispensed by God to all, laity as well as priests —this should be the goal of the exercise of priestly authority and spiritual power. Thus the Council breaks the possibility of the deadening grip of a monopolistic clericalism.*

It is interesting to compare the words of Mother Eucharia, Bishop De Roo, and Bishop Young with many

---

* Quoted from *The Documents of Vatican II,* 529.

of the traditional parishes where the pastor is the lord of creation, the curates are his obedient vassals, and the people are the voiceless serfs. The traditional parish had done its part, and done it well, in the development of American Catholicism, but times have changed, the Church has changed, and an entirely different style of ecclesiastical leadership is required not only by the dictates of the situation in which the Church finds itself but also by the Conciliar documents.

I might suggest in passing that I cannot conceive of a situation of the Church in the next couple of decades in which the relationship between pastor and curate will not be so drastically changed that the distinction will almost cease to exist. The ultimate judgment that must be made of the pastor-curate relationship is that even if it were not a violation of Christian charity, it would still have to be abandoned because of its consummate inefficiency. The relationship between pastor and curate is surely one of the most depressive and degrading relationships that has survived from the feudal ages. It severely maims the talents and the efficiency of assistants, and isolates and impedes the talents of the pastor. Historians of the future will view the pastor-curate relationship as it has existed in the United States as something one could understand in historical context, like the Spanish Inquisition, but nonetheless something of which one is greatly ashamed. We may regret its passing or rejoice in its going, but the harsh lines of the caste distinction which separates pastors from curates will shortly vanish in the Church.

One hears it said frequently that the Vatican Council has brought about a crisis of authority and obedience in the Church, but it seems that when one speaks of crisis of authority or crisis of obedience, one is using preconciliar rhetoric. We must redefine the question of authority and obedience in postconciliar terms if we are to find our way out of the dilemma that freedom versus authority apparently presents to us. We will be assisted in doing this by two concepts—first of all, the concept of the distinction between an administrator and leader, and secondly, the concept of what a teacher and a leader ought to be in modern society.

The administrator is someone who gets things done. The leader is someone who influences the minds and hearts of men. I do not want to imply that administration is unnecessary. It is extremely necessary in any complex organization, but I want to emphasize that administration, while necessary, is relatively unimportant. Unfortunately, the American clergy, partly because of the emotional immaturity discussed in the previous chapter, are frequently "hung up" on administration as though by proving themselves to be effective administrators, they could establish the validity of their claim to be an American male.

Our involvement with parochial schooling in particular

is a sign of how we turn from leadership to the security of administration. There is no reason why the administration of Catholic education ought not to be in lay hands. Catholic schools in Canada are generally administered by laity rather than by the clergy, and the pastors are free from concerns about the building and maintaining of the Catholic school system. In the United States we are often tempted to wonder what would a parish priest do if he didn't have a school to consume his time. We American Catholics are probably the best administrators in the world, and that is a good thing because the Catholic Church in other countries could desperately stand some of our administrative efficiency. But we American Catholic clergy must come to realize that administration is not enough and that while the American Church has through its history been long on administration, it has all too frequently been short on leadership (although we must not overlook the great leaders of the Church—men like Carroll, England, Hughes, Keane, Gibbons, and Ireland).

What then is a leader, and what is a teacher? It would be very interesting for all who exercise leadership either as pastors or assistants to read Eli Abell's book on the missile crisis and study carefully the behavior of John Kennedy in relationship to the Executive Committee of the National Security Council during the crisis. Kennedy did not make by himself the decision of how the missile crisis was to be contained. Indeed, he refused even to attend many of the meetings of the Executive Committee because he felt that his presence would prevent his colleagues from expressing their opinions forcefully enough. It was only when a broad general consensus had been reached among his advisors that Kennedy began to sit in on the discussion and formulate the specific details of the execution of the collegial decision. This is not to say that the decision was not his. Obviously it was. But he achieved the decision only through a collegial, consensus-producing operation, and he did everything in his power to facilitate the broadest possible freedom of expression on the part of his colleagues in order that the strongest possible consensus might be fashioned. This is precisely how a leader operates in the modern world. He influences the minds and hearts of men by permitting their minds and hearts to influence him.

Groups of highly skilled professionals generally come together to work as a group because of the "economies" involved. By this term is meant not merely the shared financial expenses but even more the shared talents, competencies, training, and resources. In most such circumstances whatever authority the senior colleague has comes from the consent of his confreres, though they may bind themselves to accept his decisions.

The principal function of the senior colleague in such a collegium is to create a climate in which his colleagues will be able to operate with maximum productivity. He must do all in his power to see that the various resources and talents which the different members of the college can bring to bear are developed to their fullest and given the greatest possible opportunity to function. He makes sure that the physical environment is conducive to effective work, provides the college with the tools and materials the respective members need, mediates the communication flow and interaction patterns among the membership to keep tensions at a minimum, and, most important, provides the vision of the common goal which the individual members may lose sight of in their own personal commitments. He also acts as a catalyst whose own ideas and insights will stir up the creative processes in his colleagues. His leadership is essentially one of service and vision. He must be ready to listen constantly, and react constructively and reassuringly to the ideas of his associates. When it is necessary for him to take the initiative, he does so only after careful consultation with his colleagues because he knows that unilateral and unexpected action on his part will not only cause consternation and demoralization among his colleagues, but it will also seriously impair the effectiveness of his initiative. His approach to his colleagues is one of posing questions and presenting problems rather than preparing prefabricated answers.

A special psychological orientation is necessary for the senior colleague to play this role. He must honestly believe that his colleagues can do most things better than he can and that his function is to facilitate the action of their skills. He must be convinced that there is no problem which the college faces that he can solve by himself without their assistance and collaboration. He must be firmly and patiently committed to the need for consultation and conversation, and take it as unquestioned that the college cannot move (at least in any dramatic fashion) without broad consensus among the membership. He must understand that only the maximum commitment of energy and talent from his colleagues will enable the college to achieve its goals and that unless he guarantees to them the greatest possible amount of initiative and responsibility, they will not be able to make the required commitment. He must see his function not as giving orders, but rather as obtaining commitment and consent.

It is obvious, of course, how this model of professional collegiality applies to the work of the priests of the Church—the bishop with his pastors, the pastors with their assistants, and all the ministers of the Church with the People of God. When we stop to think about it long enough, we may even come to understand that this is how the Lord dealt with his twelve apostles.

In similar fashion, we can reevaluate the meaning of the word teacher. In his brilliant book, *Toward A Contemporary Christianity*, Brian Wicker thinks that much of the problem the modern world finds in the Church's

self-description as a teacher flows from a fact which the
Church does not yet fully understand, that the concept
of teaching has drastically changed from that of the pro-
fessor who imparts knowledge to the students eagerly
scribbling in a notebook to a much more sophisticated
notion of the teacher as the one who presides over the
seminar.

It is to the notion of the seminar, not to that of the classroom
or the lecture hall, that we must look for our analogies. The
classroom suggests immaturity, the lecture hall impersonality
and one-sidedness. It is in the seminar, where the teacher's
role is that of catalyst, the crystallizer of the thoughts of the
group, that a suitable context can be found for a new theological exploration of the concept of the teaching church, and
of the bishop as "tutor" to his "students." The initiative may
come from any member of the group. Discussion is free-rang-
ing and uninhibited. But it is not without direction. For the
tutor's task is to give a sense of direction; to point out the
ideas which have been forgotten, the emphases which are out
of balance, the facts which have been misstated or misused,
the arguments which are invalid or lacking in evidential support. His authority for doing this lies partly in his position as
the acknowledged and appointed tutor, and partly in his superior knowledge of the subject and skill in handling difficulties. His authority is not given to him by the group; but in
order to maintain the credibility of his position, he must con-
tinually vindicate his authority by the evidence of his com-

petence, his sensitivity to the interests of the students, his capacity to stimulate them to new ideas, and his general awareness of the context in which the group's work is being carried on. He must be both a traditionalist and a contemporary, living at the edges where new life comes into being, on the boundaries between past and future.

This, I suggest, is the best model available for the structure of a human community which is dedicated primarily to the exploration of experience and the increase of self-awareness. It is on this structure that the other teaching processes—the imparting of facts, the supervision of experiments, the conducting of research—all focus; for it is here that the creative work of a learning community is carried on. Indeed since teaching (as opposed to proclaiming) implies learning as its other term, the very concept of a teaching church implies that of a learning church. The two cannot be separated; for they are simply the opposite sides of a single process of self-exploration by the whole people of God. As Abbot Butler has said in reviewing Hans Küng's *Structures of the Church:* "We shall have to think again about any distinction between *ecclesia docens* and *ecclesia discens.* These are, perhaps, rather two aspects of a single entity."*

Wicker then makes a very interesting comparison between the seminar and the liturgy. He points out how

* Brian Wicker, *Toward A Contemporary Christianity* (Notre Dame, 1967), 274–275, with full credit to University of Notre Dame Press.

much liturgy is really like a seminar in structure and, therefore, how suggestive it is on the subject of the Church and the priest as teacher.

If I may make a personal comment as someone who has presided both over lectures and over seminars, the latter is a far more effective way of teaching. In fact, he who presides over a seminar has far more authority and impact on his students than he who stands before them on a lecture podium in an authoritarian manner and teaches them what is truth.

I want to emphasize that neither the social organization theory of collegiality nor Wicker's theory of the Church as seminar teacher calls into question in any fashion the nature of authority, but it simply emphasizes that which we should never have forgotten. The authority of the Church and the authority of the priest is an authority which implies service and understanding, the responsibility of acting as a catalyst and of presenting vision, the responsibility of bringing to the community excitement, interest, precision, and charity. This is what a truly great teacher is, and this is what any priest who aspires to be a teacher must strive to be.

Let no one argue that the talents of leadership or teaching which I have described are beyond their reach. These talents are not at all innate. Some people, indeed, have more natural inclinations to be good teachers and good leaders than others, but the ability to preside over a seminar or to preside over the Eucharist in charity is the ability any one of us can acquire with courage, trust, and diligence. The young priest who argues that there is no reason why he should be a community leader more than anybody else because he has no greater talents than anybody else in the community for leadership forgets completely that leadership and teaching are roles, not inborn talents, and anyone can learn the behavior required by the role. We need not be Pied Pipers; we need simply to be intelligent, open, and courageous human beings.

This then is how the priest fulfills his role of building up the Christian community. The priest is the teacher, the leader, the president who serves the Eucharistic community in charity.

For through the apostolic proclamation of the gospel, the People of God is called together. . . . They cannot be ministers of Christ unless they are witnesses and dispensers of a life other than this earthly one. But they cannot be of service to men if they remain strangers to the life and conditions of men. . . . The Eucharistic Action is the very heartbeat of the congregation of the faithful over which the priest presides. . . . Priests must sincerely acknowledge and promote the dignity of the laity. . . . They should scrupulously honor that just freedom which is due to everyone in this earthly city. They should listen to the laity willingly, consider their wishes in a fraternal spirit, and recognize their experience and competence in the different areas of human activity, *so that together with* *them they will be able to read the signs of the times.* While testing spirits to see if they be of God, priests should discover with the instinct of faith, acknowledge with joy, and foster with diligence the various humble and exalted charisms of the laity. . . . priests have been placed in the midst of the laity to lead them to the unity of charity, that they may "love one another with fraternal charity, anticipating one another with honor" (Rom. 12:10). It is their task, therefore, to reconcile differences of mentality in such a way that no one will feel himself a stranger in the community of the faithful.*

The Vatican Council leaves little doubt as to what the role of the priest really is, nor I think can we be in much doubt that we have a long way to go before we live up to this deal. It is going to take us awhile to reach the ideal but at least we can begin to try. An interesting exercise for us to consider intellectually is the question of how, in the framework of the Conciliar documents, the modern notions about the collegiality of professionals, and Brian Wicker's concept of the new teacher, we would handle the race problem within our parishes. I would say two things: an authentic collegial seminar and presiding-in-charity approach to those in our midst who are racial bigots would be an extraordinarily difficult venture, but I would also suggest that this may be the only way that the deep-seated personality problems at the root of racial prejudice can be removed. All we know in sociology and

* Quoted from *The Documents of Vatican II*, 535–553.

psychology would assure us that the style of leadership which I have outlined is the only way we know that the problem of deep-seated prejudice can be resolved. In any event, it is certainly far better in the long run than showing people movies about human relations.

4

The Priest as
the "Love Person" in
the Christian Community

SOME TIME AGO I was in the common room of a famous North American Catholic college listening to some of the younger clergy from the faculty discussing, as befits new breeders, the importance of love in human fulfillment. The president of the college stopped momentarily to listen to the conversation and shook his head with patent mystification. "I don't know what's got into you people," he said, "I've heard too much about this 'love stuff.' I really don't understand what you're talking about. I always thought that love is something that the priest has given up, and I think you people are wasting your time talking about it."

As an empirical statement of fact, the president's observation was probably correct, but, as an ideal, it would not be too much to suggest that his position is heretical, for love is at the core of Christian life, and the priest who has given up love has turned himself into both a human and a Christian zombie who will be a failure as a human being and is a failure as a priest. The academic distinction between love and charity is surely invalid in practice, especially since the latter usually comes to mean something disembodied, angelic, ethereal, and not particularly human. This ethereal, disembodied love that we call charity is hardly an accurate reflection of the behavior of the Lord who loved John the Apostle so much as to permit him to rest his head upon his chest, or loved Mary Magdalene so much as to permit her to wash his feet with her tears, or the Lord who loved Lazarus so much that he would cry out in pain at the news of his death, or the Lord who loved his Father's house so much that he would cast money changers out of the temple and damn the hypocrisy of the Pharisees. When the Lord loved, he loved not with an angelic charity but with a powerful, profound, and passionate human love.

One of the parishes at which I was stationed was once denounced to the Holy Office for preaching strange and unusual doctrines. It turned out on investigation that the occasion for the denunciation was a passage from the new Confraternity translation of the Acts of the Apostles in which Peter refers to the Lord as "the man Jesus." So dehumanized has Jesus become in the minds of some

Christians that even a translation approved by the American bishops which refers to him as a man is deemed worthy of denunciation to the Holy Office. Something has gone radically wrong with our notions of the Lord.

It is idle to assay a definition of love, but we can at least describe it as a gift of self to another without the loss of self. It is, in the words of Martin D'Arcy, not the desire to possess but to be possessed by the beloved. Of course such a desire first presuppses that one possesses oneself because one cannot give that which one does not have. This desire to be possessed by the beloved has as its goal the expectation that such possession will make the other happy. In such a framework one must love oneself and trust the other. One must be willing to run the risk of being rejected, of getting hurt. Trusting someone else with our person is a most dangerous and painful virtue, and yet it is one without which we cannot be human. On the phenomenological level original sin is precisely the inability to trust others, the inability to give oneself in love. It is this lack of trust as the prelude to love which Christ came to heal. The disunity which existed in the world before the Lord's coming was a disunity based on distrust and the inability to give oneself to others in love. Christ healed this disunity by giving himself for our salvation because of his love for us; by this gift of himself he formed a new community in which men could be themselves and give themselves in love even at the risk of destruction. The result of Christ's gift of himself in love to his community is that slowly and gradually the wounds of self-hatred, suspicion, distrust, and fear which separate men are being healed.

The Eucharist is the ritual reenactment of the Lord's gift of himself as well as a celebration of the unity and love which unites all Christians (it might be noted how pathetic the liturgy often is as this kind of sign of loving unity, especially the old baroque-style solemn Mass with the various ministers snarling at each other *sotto voce* about violations of the detailed rubrical protocol). If the role of the priest is to spread warmth and affection among the People of God, and if his presidency of the Eucharistic community is the core of this role, it would follow that we can judge how effective he is by the way the liturgy is performed. God help us if the typical Sunday liturgy is the measure of the generosity and love and concern we bring to the Christian community.

A priest then is the one who presides over the Eucharist and over the Eucharistic community which in fact are the same. He makes Christ once again present in the Eucharist; by his life of building up the Christian community he becomes Christ for his people not only in the heart of the Eucharistic assembly but also in his own personal giving of himself in loving service to his people.

How does he exercise his presidency in love which is a presidency of self-giving? The Conciliar documents give us a hint of an answer. The priest is to be, in the community, the absorber of hatred, suspicion, and distrust; by his own skills of leadership and by the virtues of his life he is to create an atmosphere of charity wherein the People of God need not be afraid to be themselves and to give of themselves, because their priest has already given of himself. The priest as president of the Eucharistic community must create an atmosphere of warmth, kindness, generosity, openness, and concern. It is his task *ex officio* to teach others how to love by loving himself. Again, let me stress that it is not necessarily a natural talent. It is not an ability that some people are born with and others acquire. There may be experiences in our background that will enable some of us to do this more readily than others, but no one who is human can claim to be incapable of giving himself to others in love. While trust may be something that is natural to a little child, it is lost by virtually all of us as we grow to maturity and must be reacquired by practice and effort.

It is particularly easy to lose our ability to trust when we live in a situation of suspicion and distrust, a situation which characterized the seminary training that most of us received. Because the seminary authorities did not trust us, they created situations in which we were really unable to trust our fellows; hence, we all built the defense mechanisms which kept a hostile and suspicious world at bay. Furthermore, relationships in the rectory all too fre-

quently are primarily relationships of distrust and suspicion, a suspicion which, be it noted, we may try to
cover up in the presence of lay people but which at least
in our day and age deceives none of them. It is often
ludicrous to watch a pastor try and persuade his parishioners by word and behavior that he and his assistants
form one great big happy family. Even if the parishioners
did not know better from their own experience, the
artificiality of the phony cordiality that some pastors
exhibit on public occasions is patent. If you really are
not able to trust others, you will not be very good at
pretending that you can.

The priest, particularly the parish priest, is held to love
and trust *ex officio*. It is for this purpose that he is or-
dained and sent to his people, and the Christian community cannot do without his priestly love. In its absence
the community, that is to say the community which cele-
brates its unity in communion, simply will not flourish
because he who is to be the center of their communion
refuses to unite himself with those around him. He hides
behind his Roman collar, his clericalist manners, his membership in the privileged caste, and the patently artificial
wit and good humor which so many priests erect as a
barrier to keep other human beings away from their
battered, insecure, and threatened little egos. God will
forgive those who trained us because they acted in good
faith, but it must be said that many did everything in

their power to see that we were precisely not the kind of human beings that the People of God would require.

The Conciliar documents speak of the "servant Church," and there has always been a lot of happy talk—especially among those in positions of authority—about the clergy as servants. But if we are servants, then surely we are the most unusual servants the world has ever seen: loaded with privileges and prerogatives and titles and fancy robes. We might do well to ponder the core meaning of being a servant: the good servant is concerned completely with the happiness, welfare, convenience, and freedom of the one whom he serves and would not think of acting for his master without making certain he knew his wishes. I would submit that most of us are not very good servants and that we rather expect to be served than to serve. Nor do we have to look very far for evidence of how high and mighty some of the clergy have made themselves. They are not servants; they are, rather, the masters and everyone had better remember it.

The love that is required of the priest, as he presides in love over the Christian people, is a love that will require him to become deeply and profoundly involved in his people's lives. Indeed, affection toward another which does not involve profound concern is hardly worthy of the title of love. It, therefore, follows that the priest must be "attached" to his people. We were warned in the seminary about the dangers of attachment and involve-

ment. It was pointed out to us that if we became emotionally involved with our people, it would be a serious
threat to our vocation and to the unselfishness of our
service of the Lord—as though one could serve him without loving the least of his brothers. Emotional attachment
and involvement with any person has some elements of
danger to it. There is always the risk that our emotions
will trick us and will sweep us away so that we lose control and possession of ourself. But he who rejects human
emotions because they are risky, he who rejects human
involvement because it could be dangerous, rejects the
possibility of human life. Life itself is a risk and a danger,
and he who wishes to play it safe, to avoid all risks involved, chooses not to live at all.

The real risk and the real peril is not that we will
become emotionally involved with our people but rather
that our emotional involvement with them will not really
be that of unselfish love. It is much easier to form mutual
dependency relationships which, far from liberating our
people from fear and distrust, enslave them all the more
to insecurity and anxiety. It is so very easy to deceive
ourselves into thinking that what we feel is unselfish love
when what we are engaged in is a form of sophisticated
and subtle exploitation of people's needs and weaknesses
to satisfy the powerful hunger of our own neurotic needs
and dependencies. Priests are especially good at this kind
of manipulation, particularly in dealing with the hero-

worshipping tendencies of young people. Because of the great esteem of our position, because of the great respect young people feel for us as priests, we can readily become surrogate father figures in their lives. We then use this position, almost mercilessly, to make them dependent on our smile and our approval and our encouragement for all their major decisions.

Furthermore, in this age of the more sophisticated kinds of manipulation that group dynamics make possible, we can reduce our people to a state of emotional dependency on us while at the same time proclaiming that they are freer than ever before. We can use a pretext of honesty and openness as a subtle weapon for aggression and imprisonment and deceive ourselves into thinking that we are not feeding the insatiable hunger of neurosis. Because we have never grown mature enough to be able to love and permit ourselves to be loved (in some way a more frightening experience than loving), we have great needs for affection. We surround ourselves with worshipping followers whose neurotic adoration is temporarily a reassurance to us that we do have a value and a worth (though in the depths of our souls doubt persists).

The tendency to manipulate others is strong, and especially strong in those of us who, by reason of temperament or vocation, have chosen careers which require that we deal constantly with people. It is an extraordinarily serious responsibility to become deeply involved in the problems, the fears, the hopes, the expectations, and the sorrows of our fellow human beings. If we choose to do it as our vocation in life—and every parish priest has surely chosen it—then we must beware of the dangers and the temptations that are involved in such a choice.

We dare not approach our people in a shallow, superficial, or casual fashion because we are the ones who preside in love over the People of God. We are capable of doing great good for them. If we can generate an atmosphere of warmth and trust and confidence in the community we serve, then we continue the work of the Lord. If we keep our people at a distance from us and react to them in a cold, indifferent, and aloof manner, we are impeding and slowing down the work of the Lord and proving false to our priestly vocation. But if we create an atmosphere of pseudo-trust and phony honesty and counterfeit love which, far from freeing our people from suspicion and distrust, rather enslaves them to our own neurotic needs, then we are perverting our mission as president of the Christian people, and are trying to push back the Lord's work. God forgive us if we do this, at least if we do it out of any other motivation save the crassest kind of ignorance.

If we evaluate our relationships with our people in the terms of the ideal of warmth, openness, service, and trust described in the preceding paragraphs, we must acknowledge that we have been something short of complete

successes. For all the talk about charity during our seminary experiences (and we probably heard more about
obedience than we did about charity), there was precious
little in those years that prepared us for anything remotely resembling mature human love. The infantile sus-
picions, distrusts, and rivalries which permeate so many
rectories are hardly calculated to create an atmosphere in
which our capacity of love would increase. We are generous with our time, our energy, our money, and our effort,
but there is one thing we are not generous with and that
is ourselves. We really do not want to run the risk of
putting aside our defense mechanisms and being at the
mercy of the affection of our people. Indeed, if we even
begin to attempt this, the experience can be so frightening and so overwhelming that we very quickly flee
from it.

It is easy for us to find rationalizations about having
given up love when we chose celibacy. We can fall back
on clichés about the dangers of attachment and involvement and of losing our hearts to our people. Hide behind
these rationalizations if we must, but we still should not
deceive ourselves with the thought that they represent
piety or virtue. They are, rather, defense mechanisms,
expressions of fear, insecurity, and self-hatred. That they
have come to be accepted as signs of virtue is evidence
of how completely we have forgotten the central message
of Christianity and how much the Manichean tradition

has managed to seep into our faith and our training. We need only look at many of the priests we know to realize that, in spite of all their work and generosity, they are frightened of really loving their people and permitting them to love them in return. Worship and admiration from a distance is fine, but human love up close is terrifying. So priests grow old hiding behind their Roman collars, crouching in fear behind the altar, defining inhumanity as piety, and refusing to let that which is most noble in them emerge. As their physical strength begins to fail, they become confused, lonely, frustrated, sterile old men who have never loved and never permitted themselves to be loved in return. They are terrified at the usually repressed thought that their harsh and cold lives may not have been after all a precise imitation of the pattern set down by Jesus of Nazareth.

5

The Priest as Man of Hope and Vision

NORTON LONG, one of the most astute political scientists in America, has an interesting theory about the role of the political leader in which he describes the top executive of a city, state, or nation as an "uncertainty absorber." Any major important decision that an organization makes is bound to involve a large number of imponderables. Even though the decision has been reached collegially and on the basis of a broad consensus, it nonetheless cannot be based entirely on demonstrated certainties. It is, therefore, the task of the leader of the organization, because he has a clear vision of the organization's goals, to radiate the confidence and the optimism necessary to sustain the organization through times of doubt and uncertainty.

We can see what this theory of the leader as "uncertainty absorber" means more clearly in practice if once again we turn to the 1962 missile crisis. The decision of the Executive Committee of the National Security Council was nearly unanimous. Everyone agreed that the graduated response to the aggressive Soviet actions was the wisest possible course. Yet when John Kennedy went on television to explain this decision to the nation, his task was not at all primarily to persuade the American public of the careful wisdom of his administration's contingency planning. His role, rather, was to reassure them that what was being done could be integrated into the vision of the goals of American society, that there was reason for hope and confidence, and that brave and careful action would see us through times of grave peril. The "uncertainty absorber" is not a man who deceives his followers, not a man who hides the truth from them or offers grounds for optimism that do not exist. He absorbs uncertainty not by deception but rather by offering vision and hope. This is the role of a leader in any organization, and this is also the role of the priest to the People of God.

He must bring hope to the Christian faithful, and hope in its turn depends on vision. The priest must be a seer of what the implications are in every new development within his people. He must be a prophet of the vision of the life ahead. I do not mean simply continued life after the illusion of death but also the life of trust and love in the Christian community before death. Without faith in the possibility of this vision and without hope that it can in some fashion be achieved, the Christian community cannot long survive. It needs the priest's vision and the priest's hope to hold it together.

We must stress again in this context that to be a prophet, a seer of a vision, a man of hope, requires no special inborn talents; like love and leadership, it is rather an ability that all of us have and which all of us are capable of developing. Anyone who dares to assume the role of president of the Eucharistic community is *ex officio* held to be a man of hope. He must bring hope to his people, just as Christ came into the world to bring hope. We need only turn to the Last Supper discourse to his apostles to see how much hope the Lord did bring them:

Let not your heart be troubled; if you believe in God you believe also in me. In my Father's house there are many mansions; if not I would have told you, because I go to prepare a place for you, and if I go to prepare a place for you I will come again and will take you to myself, that where I am you may also be . . . peace I leave with you, my peace I give unto you, not as the world giveth do I give unto you. Let not your heart be troubled, do not let it be afraid . . . these things I have spoken to you that my joy may be in you and your joy may be filled.

It was not, however, an unrealistic hope:

I say to you that you shall weep but that the world shall rejoice, and you shall be made sorrowful but your sorrow shall
be turned into joy. . . . I pray not that thou shouldst take them
out of the world, but that thou shouldst keep them from evil.
. . . That they all may be one; as thou, Father, art in me, and
I in thee, that they also may be one in us: that the world may
believe that thou hast sent me. . . . Father, I will that they also
whom thou hast given me be with me where I am; that they
may see my glory which thou hast given me.

The Lord, then, did not promise his followers that they
would be free from pain or suffering. He did not take a
shallow superficial stance toward reality by denying the
possibility of pain or suffering, much less by covering it
up with a shallow optimism and a ready wisecrack. He
offered hope which did not ignore evil, but hope which
would persist in spite of evil. The priest who wishes to
know what the proper rhetoric is for hope in time of
trouble and difficulty would do well to reread the Last
Supper discourse, or John Kennedy's speech to the United
States at the time of the missile crisis, or Pope John's
opening address at the Vatican Council—especially when
he grows discouraged about the complexities and ambiguities of change.

In the daily exercise of our pastoral office, we sometimes have
to listen, much to our regret, to voices of persons who, though
burning with zeal, are not endowed with too much sense of

discretion or measure. In these modern times they can see nothing but prevarication and ruin. They say that our era, in comparison with past eras, is getting worse, and they behave as though they had learned nothing from history, which is, none the less, the teacher of life. They behave as though at the time of former Councils everything was a full triumph for the Christian idea and life and for proper religious liberty.

We feel we must disagree with those prophets of doom, who are always forecasting disaster, as though the end of the world were at hand.

In the present order of things, Divine Providence is leading us to a new order of human relations which, by men's own efforts and even beyond their very expectations, are directed toward the fulfillment of God's superior and inscrutable designs. And everything, even human differences, leads to the greater good of the Church.

We may well contrast the hopeful and visionary style of the Lord, of President Kennedy and Pope John, with the prophets of doom in our own midst. Almost every week the Catholic press has some new statement in which an ecclesiastical authority warns us of disaster just around the corner. The prophets of doom by no means gave up their wailing when Pope John expressed his regret in having to listen to them. We would be deceiving ourselves if we did not think that there were many rectory

supper tables across the length and breadth of our re-
public that do not have their own prophets of doom
whose cynicism, immaturity, and pessimism blind them
both to the possibility of hope and to their own *ex officio*
responsibility to be men of vision.

In time of crisis and ambiguity it is utter disaster to
any organization if its leadership loses its nerve. Hence,
there can be no greater affliction in the contemporary
Church than if the clergy lose their courage, their confidence, and their vision. Heaven save us from priests
who stand around wringing their hands and moaning because they do not know what is coming of the world, or
what they, as priests, ought to be, or whether there is
anything left to be done except patiently await disaster.
When the clergy abandon their role as men of confidence
and vision and hope, then no one is minding the store and
no one has his hand on the tiller; the store will be robbed,
and the boat will be capsized, and the flock will disperse
because it has lost its shepherd.

The prophets of doom can be found both in the older
clergy and in the younger clergy. The senior prophets of
doom lament that things are not like they used to be,
that adults are not so generous, children so docile, and all
Catholics not so loyal as they were in the good old days.
The senior prophets are right about one thing; things
surely are not what they used to be, and the changes
have only begun. But the senior prophets of doom con-

fuse their own bewilderment and immaturity with the world outside themselves. Because things are going badly for them, they argue that things are going badly for the Church, and they refuse to heed the message of hope that the Council Fathers and the Popes have offered us. They know better—these prophets of doom—they know that the world is going to pieces and they are not prepared to look at any contrary evidence.

The junior prophets of doom take a much different approach. Their technique is to make exhibitionistic fools out of themselves, to demonstrate to anyone who is patient enough to listen to them how they are filled with self-pity and angst and insoluble identity crises. In the younger prophets of doom a constant affirmation that they do not know the meaning of the priestly role is a marvelous excuse for inactivity, for the avoidance of risk-taking, and for getting the attention and sympathy which their immature personalities passionately crave. They will not look to the Conciliar documents for guidance on what the priestly role is; neither will they listen to anyone who is older than they. They must solve the problems themselves, and they have defined the terms of solution in such a way that the problems will be permanently insoluble. For all their youthful vigor and personalistic jargon, their net impact on the People of God is the same as that of the senior prophets of doom. They cheat their

people of the vision and hope that the people have a right
to demand.

These are not easy times, and while the signs of the
times are generally encouraging, one would be gravely
mistaken if he did not see serious problems and difficulties
on all sides. Nor would one be realistic if one did not
admit that there is much less clarity now than there used
to be about what specific activities the priest should be
engaged in. The Conciliar documents offer us clear guidelines, but it is not going to be particularly easy to apply
these guidelines in practice. However, hope is only a
virtue in uncertain circumstances. If it were clear what
we should be doing, and if it were clear that we would
overcome all the obstacles around us, then we would
have certainty and there would be no need for hope. As
Gilbert Chesterton wisely remarked, "Hope is only a
virtue when the situation is hopeless." Our situation at
present is anything but hopeless, but there is enough confusion, uncertainty, and danger in it that the Christian
people must have hope, and lots of it. If they do not receive this hope from their leaders and their priests, then
where are they to look for hope? If the salt of the earth
loses its savor, what good is it save to be thrown out and
trampled underfoot?

It is not required of us that we know all the answers,
and it is long past time that we all put aside the strange
notion, which we acquired in the seminary, that there was

an answer for almost every problem, and that the parish priest was expected not only to know this answer but to provide it immediately for everyone who came to him seeking it. Instead of being answer-men, we are guides on a pilgrimage. We do not know exactly where we are going, but we can point out to our people the general direction of our journey. Our visions of what the goal is like may be vague, but they also must be splendid. We must be able to persuade our people that it is possible for man to grow in unity and in friendship and love, and, indeed, that the Lord's coming into the world guaranteed the ultimate victory of unity and love over fear, hatred, dissension, conflict, and distrust. We must further persuade them that mankind's pilgrimage toward freedom and love is continuing in spite of all the setbacks, all the disasters, all the mishaps, all the horrendous blunders. The human race moves slowly forward with the Church struggling once again for the only place in the pilgrimage that it would not be ashamed to hold—a place in the vanguard, the leading edge of man's journey toward the Omega point.

The charisma of hope and vision is, of course, not the sole property of the priest, though he is held to it *ex officio*. There are other members of the Christian community who have perhaps in far greater abundance than priests the charisma of hope and vision. He who presides in charity over the community must listen carefully for their voices of vision and hope. He must encourage them to speak out, to tell the rest of the people why they should have confidence and courage and what is the nature of the destination of their pilgrimage. As he who searches out charisma and judges the operations of the Holy Spirit, the priest must be acutely conscious of how necessary it is to join his own hope, his own vision, to the hope and vision of others.

But the question remains, why should we hope? Is not the world an evil and ugly place in which sin and hatred and death abound, where millions can be killed in concentration camps and hundreds of thousands obliterated in one flash of a nuclear bomb? Can one indeed see much reason for hope in the evil, suffering, and misery that remain in the world? To this we must reply that seldom in human history has there been so much reason for hope, despite all the contrary evidence for despair. On the natural level we see that mankind is converging, and the increasing size of the human race combined with the fantastic progress in transportation and communication has led to the humanization of the planet. We are now all neighbors, all parts of a village around whose limits man can walk in space within three hours, or, to put the matter somewhat differently, as Barbara Ward has done, we can now speak of spaceship-earth.

With this new found unity of the human race there has also come far greater control of the physical environment in which we live. It is technically possible now, for the first time in history, to eliminate many forms of sickness, almost all forms of hunger, and even, if we put our minds to it, most varieties of physical poverty. Our social organizations have not kept up with our technical skills, but here too we are making progress. We are on the verge of major breakthroughs in our understanding of the dynamics of human nature and the processes by which men relate to their fellowmen. We understand the underlying causes of distrust and fear. Even though our therapeutic resources for dealing with these terrible evils have scarcely proceeded beyond the stage at which physical medicine was when it used herbs and incantations, we have at least made a beginning. The physical humanization of the planet is but a prelude to the social and psychological humanization of the planet. There is still a long, long way to go before the barriers which separate a man from his fellowman can be completely eliminated, but only the most gloomy pessimist would deny that progress has been made.

If on the natural level there are grounds for hope, on the religious level there are even more powerful reasons. One need only look about him, travel a bit in the American Church or throughout the Catholic world, to sense that the Spirit is abroad in the land blowing always as he will, but also blowing as he never has before in the whole life of the Church. The action of the Spirit among us is quickening at a fantastic pace. All around us there is an outpouring of theology and of Christian concern, the like of which we have never seen before. One would be ill-advised to predict, on the basis of the present circumstances, a new religious golden age—if indeed there ever was an old religious golden age—but we can at least say that enthusiasm, vigor, excitement, and commitment flourish all around us. If they do not always flourish in the style to which we have been accustomed, or the manner which our prejudices deem most appropriate, the fault may frequently be with us. It could be that we are not docile to the Spirit, that we do not hear him as he sweeps by us, and that many of those around us, even those who are not Christians, may actually hear the voice of the Spirit more readily than we do.

But if there is reason for hope, both naturally and religiously, there is no evidence of certainty. Ours are troubled times, and the signs of the times are frequently obscure. If they were not, then there would be no need for hope. But there is need for hope. The People of God need it greatly. What do they receive when they turn to us, their men of vision and hope? Often they find that we are even less hopeful than they because we have lost our nerve, our courage, and our vision, and have given up. We have abdicated our prophetic role.

6

The Priest and Freedom

SEVERAL YEARS AGO I was assigned to give a talk at a priests' retreat on the question of the priest and freedom. It was expected of me that, since this was a very liberal retreat group, I would talk about our own freedom and the abuse of authority on the part of those who are our superiors. Rather perversely, perhaps, I chose rather to speak about freedom of others in relationship to us. Instead of attacking pastors' abuse of authority, I pointed out that almost all of us priests are constantly under temptation to abuse the authority of the position we occupy. I noted that only when one generation of curates is conscious that it can so readily misuse its position to deprive others of freedom, can we expect the next generation of pastors to also be that conscious, and that if a man abuses his position as a pastor, it was because he did it as a curate, too. I cited with approval J. F. Power's classic definition of a curate as a mouse in training to be a rat, and then pointed out that whether we be pastor or curate was irrelevant. The way we use authority and the way we treat other people's freedom is a matter of a basic personality orientation which is little affected, save in some of its external manifestations, by the particular role we occupy. My colleagues at the retreat listened dutifully to my remarks, and there was a lengthy discussion period afterward. What do you think we talked about? The answer should not be difficult to guess. We talked about our pastors.

The tragic problem is that for all our words about the proper use of authority and respect for freedom, there is so much in our background and training that militates against the proper use of authority. We can only with tremendous difficulty avoid the temptation of abusing the position of our office to limit the freedom of others.

First, there is the conviction many of us have absorbed, through long years of being subject to it, that virtue can be trained by compulsion. For example, we have come to believe that habits of frequent confession can be developed by herding grammar school children into the Church on the Thursday morning before first Friday and passing them through the confessional much as IBM cards are run through a computer. Some of us believe

that respect in the Eucharistic worship can be furthered
by compelling young people to attend church either daily
or frequently. In Catholic colleges and universities we are
only reluctantly giving up the notion that compulsory
religious life, compulsory retreats, and compulsory theology courses are the ways to develop virtuous lay adults.
We still are not persuaded that compulsory attendance
at convert instructions is a horrendous abuse of personal
freedom, nor are we ready to believe that severe moral
pressures on parents and children toward attendance at
C.C.D. instructions may do more harm than good. We
were brought up in an atmosphere of compulsion, force,
and pressure employed as a shortcut for developing virtue. Since we were trained under compulsion, it is terribly difficult for us to give up the notion that compulsion
develops virtue.

The arguments for compulsory virtue are weak and
shabby. We hear it said that if young people learn good
religious habits through force when they are in school,
they will maintain these habits in adult life. The empirical
data are strong that this does not work; but we should
not need empirical data. St. Thomas assures us that virtue
is developed by the repetition of free human acts. If acts
are free, they are not compelled, and if they are compelled, they are not free. The notion that compulsory
religious behavior in childhood will lead to free religious
behavior in adult life is superstitious nonsense. And the

same judgment must be passed on the notion that if you forced someone to attend, for example, an annual retreat, he will, once he gets to the retreat, begin to enjoy it and will in the course of the retreat make, as one college dean told me, "at least one good confession a year." Anyone who has even the slightest smattering of psychology knows that the possibilities of something beginning under compulsion and ending up as a result of free choice are very thin indeed, and that the result of such compulsion is that it is more likely to turn people against the thing that is compelled rather than to make them sympathetic toward it. We need only to talk to Catholic college students about their annual retreats to see that the compulsory retreat has been a disaster for the retreat movement in the United States. The notion that the compulsory retreat leads to one good confession a year betrays extraordinarily naive theology of the sacrament of penance.

Recently two young people and I gave a day of recollection at a Catholic college. The young man and woman were quite good and made a very strong impression on the college students in their discussions of freedom and service and love in the Church (impressions which were not vitiated even by the large number of students who approached us to make sure that their yellow cards were signed so that the computer would give them credit for the day of recollection as part of their requirements for graduation). At the Mass with which the day ended one of the officials of the school preached a sermon in which he argued that the retreat requirement was not after all so unreasonable, and simply asked that young people spend a few hours each year thinking about God. After a day of hearing about love and service the young people were once again brought back to the cold, harsh reality of the Church they knew, a Church of obligation, compulsion, and requirement. As one of my young colleagues said after the Mass was over, "We might just as well not have bothered." A Jesuit college president put the case against compulsion in religious activities in a somewhat different fashion: "Father, if St. Ignatius of Loyola knew that his spiritual exercises were to be made a requirement for graduation, he never would have founded the Society."

The second element in our inclination to abuse the freedom of others is the conviction that we know what is good for others better than they do themselves. It is so easy for us priests to become experts, to quickly and brilliantly sum up the nature of people's problems and then elaborate a facile answer to their difficulties. If they would only listen to us and do what we told them, all would be well with them. Since rarely do people disagree with us in such circumstances (and rarely, too, do they do what we suggest), we become complacent and self-satisfied in our expertise. The older we get the more we feel we know about human nature, and thus the more we think we are better qualified and able to pontificate in any and all problems that come to us. We refuse to recognize, of course, that the Spirit might operate differently than we do. We violate another's dignity and responsibility when we attempt to make his decisions for him, or to threaten or argue him out of his own decisions into our decisions, or even when we permit him to seduce us into making a decision for him that he would rather not make for himself (whether it be vocation, school, marriage, divorce, coming into the Church or going out of the Church).

It is not for us to decide for others, much less to argue with them. We should rather listen to the voice of the Spirit speaking in them and try and facilitate their understanding of what it is they want to do. This requires a great deal of respect for the integrity of our people, even if they seem uninformed, unintelligent, or unperceptive. It is very hard to maintain that respect, especially when in our judgment they are doing something manifestly wrong. But even if we do manage to save them from making a mistake in one set of circumstances, this does not assure us that at some other time they will not make an even more disastrous mistake because our wisdom is not available to them or because they have decided that they will act on their own initiative. We must permit our people to be religious adults even when they do not want to be religious adults. This involves the humble and honest admission that we cannot solve anyone else's problems and that we do not know what someone else should do better than he knows himself. The only role we can play as spiritual counselor is the role of facilitating other people's free decisions.

Thirdly, there is that most seductive and horrendous of temptations—the temptation to do good by maneuvering or manipulating people just a little bit so they might do what is right and what is "good for them." The temptation to do good and the temptation to help others can become very sophisticated in our day. We may have put aside the autocratic and obvious paternalism of the past. But if we substitute for it the sophisticated and subtle modern techniques of group dynamics or participatory democracy, then the modern paternalism really is far worse than the old paternalism, because it is easy for everyone to be deceived about what is going on. I am not arguing that group dynamics need degenerate into paternalistic manipulation, but I am observing that it can readily do so. The naive enthusiasm about group techniques betrayed by many clergy reveals a complete lack of understanding about how these techniques can be abused, particularly when they are in the hands of those whose training and background strongly inclines them to be manipulative in their behavior toward others. The cursillos, participatory democracy, sensitivity training—all contain much wisdom; but frequently in practice they play very recklessly with the dignity and the freedom of the individual human personality.

He who has the tremendous power over people that flows from the priestly position must lean over backward to meet every personality with great awe and great reverence. If we are to go to any extreme, then we must choose the extreme of having too much respect for the freedom and responsibility of the other, rather than too little. We must be suspicious of our own motivations and extraordinarily careful that we do not very subtly begin to manipulate our people. We must be particularly careful of this because of the honest realization that there is so much in our own backgrounds and experience which would predispose us toward manipulative behavior. It is a tragedy to observe that as we put aside the old brands of authoritarianism, there is a strong tendency in many of us to assume newer and more sophisticated brands of authoritarianism. If this should continue to happen, then the last state will be worse than the first. It is difficult for us to have a deep and profound respect for the personality of another when we do not have that respect for our own personality. The temptation to do good is a temptation experienced by weak and insecure human beings; a strong man has no need to do good but only the need to help others to do good for themselves.

There is finally the temptation to exercise social control

through charisma or the party line or social charm. The country seems to abound with people meddling in the lives of other people and, I might say particularly, with priests meddling in the lives of nuns and high school girls. Donning the mantle of wisdom and putting out the shingle of psychiatrist and sage, we invite people to come to us with their problems, and then we use our personal charm and our charisma or our unquestioned party line as a means to reduce them to subservience to us. The charismatic leader says, "You can be part of my social movement as long as you agree with me," and the purveyor of the party line says, "If you want to be a liberal, you've got to take a loyalty oath." There is no room to dissent from the dissension of the professional dissenter. The priest who is Pied Piper or the priest who exudes warmth and social charm can readily build a personal following that is unable to escape from his control and incapable of thinking for itself. Charisma or charm or theoretical ideology are not of themselves evil, but it is difficult for us to be honest with ourselves about the tremendous impact our position enables us to have on others, about the great care and delicacy with which we must behave if that impact is to enhance people's freedom rather than to take it away.

A particularly obnoxious aspect of the priest's abuse of his position is the frequent clerical patronizing of the religious. The deprecating use of the term "good sisters"

is only an indication of how insecure we are in our maleness and how absolutely necessary it is for us to keep
religious women in a state of subservience lest our own
position in the Church be threatened. Since Pope John
endorsed feminism in *Pacem in Terris,* we have no choice
but to respect the principle of equal rights for women,
and that includes equal rights for women religious. Honesty ought to compel us to admit that religious women
are far more alert intellectually than most of us, and are
also far more likely to have captured the spirit of renewal
in the Vatican Council and how to implement its decisions than are their brothers in the clergy. The need of
most priests to behave in a patronizing and superior way
toward religious women is an obvious manifestation of
their own immaturity and insecurity. The priest who
patronizes nuns is merely betraying the fact that he is
afraid of all women, and that the religious habit does not
so sufficiently obscure the femininity of the woman as to
reassure the priest that he need not fear.

At the root of these temptations is the inability to respect other people as persons and the tendency to use
them for our own needs, principally because we do not
respect ourselves. The line between manipulation and
creating a climate for freedom is a thin one, and so is the
line between leaving people free and refusing to be concerned about them. It is very difficult to steer a path down
these lines and if we are human we must resign ourselves

to frequent errors and mistakes. But while mistakes in this delicate area are easy and frequent, it does not mean that they are inevitable. The critical question in our behavior toward our people is whether the nature of the relationship is such that they are growing, that they are becoming more independent, that they are moving toward a situation where they can survive without us, or whether, on the contrary, they are becoming more dependent, more in need of us, and more incapable of action without our support. The crucial issue is not whether all our behavior toward our people is such that it respects their freedom and dignity; only a saint could claim this. The question is rather one of the general tone and quality of our behavior: whether, despite frequent mistakes, the basic tendency of our attitude toward others reveals respect for them and respect for ourselves.

The hardest thing for a priest to do is to listen, and yet there is no better way to grow in respect for the dignity and the freedom and the uniqueness of each personality that we encounter. We must listen, listen, listen. We must listen to the Holy Spirit as he speaks to us out of the hearts and minds of others. We must not expect to find "answers" in textbooks or even in the wisdom of our own experience, but rather in the wisdom of the reality in which the other finds himself. At a minimum, we must have a constant and abiding fear of breaking the bruised reed. In the absence of this ability to listen and this horror of injuring other people's dignity and freedom, authentic Christian leadership is impossible. For we are only good leaders when we are free ourselves, and we can only be free ourselves when we are courageous enough to let other people be free too.

7

The Priest and Celibacy

HUMAN NATURE BEING WHAT IT IS, and man's sexual instincts being as strong as they are, the subject of celibacy is one which always arouses the most interest in any conversation among priests. By the very nature of things, it is a delicate, highly complex issue, and we would be unrealistic to expect that there will be any immediate solution in the problems of our understanding of priestly celibacy. Because of the intense human instincts which are involved in the celibacy question, it is difficult to discuss celibacy without loss of balance and intelligence. The celibacy controversy as it rages today in many Catholic journals is long on intensity and feeling and apodictic certainties and short on wisdom and research and understanding. The celibacy question is the most ambiguous of

the ambiguous questions which presently surround the
life of the priest, but its very ambiguity demands that we
continue our serious attempts at clarification. It is not
enough simply to say that the problem is insoluble and
throw up our hands. We must admit that solutions do not
seem to be easy, and still strive to find them.

Let me proceed first of all by way of some preliminary
remarks to make my own position clear. First, celibacy is
not an obstacle to self-fulfillment, and marriage is no
guarantee of self-fulfillment. It seems so obvious that one
would not have to say this if the opposite were not so
frequently implied in the present controversy. If we are
not mature and happy as priests, we would not then be
mature and happy as husbands. Maturity, self-fulfillment,
and happiness have to be internal before there is any
possibility of developing these qualities in external relationships. It would be senseless to deny, of course, that
marriage can lead to great growth in maturity and fulfillment but only if the basic qualities are there to begin
with, and if they are not, then marriage is not going to
work any miracles and, indeed, is going to aggravate the
loneliness and frustrations of immaturity. The priest who
wrote in the *Saturday Evening Post* about how desperately he needed a woman to fulfill himself betrayed that
he had little respect for a woman since he would be using
her to meet his needs.

Some of the critics of ecclesiastical celibacy have even

argued that priests would be warmer, more sympathetic, more understanding human beings if they had wives. They have overlooked the obvious fact that large numbers of married men are not very successful as warm, sympathetic, and understanding human beings. They also ignore the psychological principle that if you are not an open and sympathetic person before marriage, instantaneous sex is not going to produce any very noticeable change after marriage. Despite all the popularized psychoanalytic arguments we may hear, celibacy is neither an obstacle to maturity or self-fulfillment nor a guarantee of it, and neither is sex. Human beings are closed up within themselves in fear and loneliness, not because they are not loved by a member of the opposite sex, but because they are not loved by themselves. Self-rejection, self-loathing, self-hatred will be solved neither by sex nor by marriage, but only by an understanding of what the factors were in our emotional background which make it impossible for us to accept our own goodness and virtues.

My second point is that those who wish to leave the priesthood should be free to do so with honor and with no limitations on their freedom to marry. There is no point in keeping in the priesthood those who do not want to be priests. Occasionally one hears the argument that if this freedom were granted, there might be a mass exodus from the priesthood. If that would be the case, it would be a sad commentary on the quality of priestly life and training, but I am inclined to suspect that this is not the case. I also think that the freedom to leave with honor, should one decide to leave, would enhance the dedication of those who stay, because they would not be then living as prisoners of a decision made once long ago. We would rather be in a situation where we were constantly free to renew our commitment. Renew our commitment most of us would, but it is nice to know that it would be a free renewal and not something with which we would be stuck whether we liked it or not.

Thirdly, despite the adulation they receive in certain Catholic quarters, I do not think that those who leave the priesthood are either heroes or prophetic witnesses. In my somewhat marginal position between the Church and the secular university, I frequently encounter people who are leaving the priesthood to marry, and I confess I am always jarred by the experience. I am old-fashioned enough to view someone's leaving the priesthood as a tragedy. Even if it is the best and most mature decision he has ever made in his life, there is still so much tragedy involved in the decision that I cannot help feeling profound regret over it. And I should note too that I find it very difficult to believe that these men are going to find the happiness outside the priesthood that they did not find in it. Given their background and training and the nature of their experiences as priests, I am not at all persuaded that they are going to be any happier with a wife than they were with their religious superior or pastor. I do not think the tragedy ends when they leave the priesthood.

Fourth, I think we will be deceiving ourselves if we believe that a married clergy would solve many problems in the Church. Lay liberals frequently argue that if there were married clergy, the birth control problem would have been solved long ago. To this I find myself saying perhaps, but I am not at all convinced that a married clergy would have had any impact at all in the solution of this problem. Given the structure of the Church from the 1930's to the beginning of the Vatican Council, upward communication about new social problems was so difficult that I am not sure a married clergy would have facilitated communication especially since the vast majority of parish priests and confessors were only too acutely aware of the problem and still simply incapable of communicating to the decision-makers the agony and intensity which surrounded this question. The notion that a married clergy would have facilitated the solution to the birth control issue is one of the easy platitudes with which the superficial are satisfied, but it is a highly dubious platitude.

Fifth, ought celibacy be optional in the western Church as apparently a majority of priests and a majority of Catholic laity think it should be? Obviously, the logic of the position I have taken on human freedom in other essays compels me to answer yes to this question. At least in the ideal order, celibacy ought to be optional, and it is not at all impossible that we will live to see at least some form of optional celibacy in the western Church, though one prophesies on this subject at great risk of being mistaken.

I do not subscribe to the fallacy frequently encountered in the writings of some journalists that celibacy is forced upon people. No one is bound to be a priest, and the Church certainly can legitimately require for the common good that certain preconditions be established for the reception of the priesthood. Hence, celibacy could only be described as the taking away of freedom if one argued that a person has either the right or duty to become a priest. I think such an argument would be very difficult to make. My contention, rather, is that it would be better and more appropriate if the common good of the Church could be served by a free choice of celibacy even among those who are already priests or who wish to be priests.

The problem of the option, if it were made available now, is that celibacy would not in fact be an option, and marriage would become almost obligatory for priests. We can see this possibility in the writings of the opponents of clerical celibacy. While they piously insist that they only want to introduce an option for priests, their whole attitude toward celibacy indicates that they want a married clergy and would view with suspicion any cleric who did not exercise his option by marrying. It is also clear that in the Episcopalian and the Orthodox experience the parish priest without a wife is viewed with grave skepticism and creates considerable social awkwardness in these Churches. Parenthetically, we might also take a closer look at the fate of Protestant ministers' wives and families before we decide that a married clergy is a very good idea for the western Catholic Church.

It therefore seems to me that, at the present time, introducing an optional version of celibacy in the western Church would, in fact, deprive priests or at least those becoming priests (for those of us who are now priests, it may be too late) of the freedom to be celibate. It might also deprive the Church of the very unique benefits the celibate clergy can supply the Church. The problem at the present time is that having taken celibacy for granted for a thousand years, the Church became very lax in developing the theological and psychological understanding of its meaning and purpose and function.

When the recent attack on the institution was launched, we had available no theoretical explanations that were particularly relevant for our time to justify clerical celibacy. I think we will be able to evolve these theoretical justifications only when structural reform in the Church and theological and social scientific developments enable us to understand more fully the meaning of celibacy. When this happens, I for one would be only too happy to see celibacy become optional in the western Church because I think that at that point large numbers of priests would freely choose the celibate state. Thus, we would be able to achieve two desired goals: we would be able to maintain the service to the common good that celibacy creates and also we would have an even greater degree of freedom in the Church, freedom that is especially appropriate in those of us who are to be leaders of the People of God.

Let me note in passing that my approach to celibacy is that it ought to be completely functional. That is to say, celibacy is not a good thing in itself. It is not an ideal to be sought for its own sake. It is a good only insofar as it contributes to the development of our priestly function: that is to say, the building up of the People of God. If celibacy contributes to this (and we must admit that it frequently has not), then it is a good thing. If it stands in the way of the priest's primary function of building up the People of God, then celibacy is something that is accidental, and the accidental must give place to the essential.

Why then is there celibacy? Why then might celibacy be a good thing? Here I think we are caught in the necessity of relying on our own intuitions and instincts rather than on any insight that Catholic theology or psychology has been able to offer us at the present time. My own response is to say that I have the still vague but very profound feeling that whatever good I may have done in the priesthood would have been much more difficult to do if I had had a wife and family. I have the feeling that celibacy makes possible, at least in the ideal order and to some extent even in the practical order, a greater love for more people and greater happiness in the service we offer. Oftentimes when I use this argument, the young radicals will dismiss it as just the "practical" argument in favor of celibacy. I am not quite sure what this accusation means. First of all, I do not think that there is necessarily anything wrong with practical arguments; they might indicate a sound theoretical base. I am not contending in some simpleminded fashion that it is for financial or organizational reasons that we ought to have an unmarried clergy. I am simply saying that celibacy seems to leave me freer to worry more intensively about more people, to put myself in the loving service of a far greater number of people—and in a far more intense way than I would be able to if I had a family of my own. And I will further argue that my instincts tell me that this kind of service can, if it is mature enough and generous enough and unselfish enough, bring to man greater happiness than marriage does.

There is another dimension of the "phenomenology of celibacy" that I would like to mention. One of the most important dimensions of the service of celibate love is the absence of the demand for reciprocity which marks all its relationships. For a married man, there is a critical area of the love in his life—namely his relationship with his wife—where, by the very nature of things, there has to be a demand for a response. If one's wife does not return love, it becomes increasingly difficult to sustain one's affection for her.

But the celibate loves the people he serves with a kind of love that characterizes all his life: a love which makes absolutely no demands for a response. If people do respond by loving him in return, that is fine, but he neither seeks it nor demands it. If there is no love in return at all, he will be a terribly unhappy person, for we all need to be loved. However, in practice there will always be love in return, and for this the priest is immensely grateful. But he seeks to specify neither the fact nor the style of the response. There is, therefore, a giving of self in celibate service that is more unselfish than married love can possibly be and hence, I would contend, more symbolic of the love of the Lord for us, a love which leaves us forever free not to respond. I hasten to add that this is all theory; in practice, celibate love is frequently anything but unselfish.

Celibacy might also be approached from the aspect of time. The married man must have certain amounts of time in his life that are sacred to the demands of his familial relationships. There is a segment of his time that he is not free to give in service of others. But the one who has chosen celibate love has no time which he can claim as his own (save for rest and recreation which are essential for any human). He is constantly at the service of the demands of his people and has no right to demand their time in return as service to his needs.

The radical enthusiasts for a married clergy will unquestionably dismiss these highly tentative arguments, but then they have made up their minds and no argument will sway them, not even the words of sacred scripture. Unfortunately for the Lord, he had not read Sigmund Freud when he praised celibacy. Neither in fact have many of the foes of celibacy, but they are nonetheless convinced that Freud and his followers have proved beyond all doubt that unless you have a wife, you cannot expect to be fulfilled.

Unfortunately, our training which keeps us immature and our structures which all too frequently keep us unfree prevent celibacy from flowering into full human love. The anxious curate wondering what his pastor thinks about him as he sits in his room waiting for the bell to summon him to fill out a Mass card, while every move is viewed with suspicion by his tyrannical boss—is this young man the result of a free and self-fulfilling kind of celibate love? Did he sacrifice the possibility of married happiness for the stagnant, repressed, narrow life that the rectory imposes upon him? Did he give up the possibility

of serving a family in love so that he might serve the
People of God in love only to find himself cut off, by the
system in which he is caught, from all effective and meaningful contact with most of the People of God? In the
answers to these questions we can find the basic reasons
for dissatisfaction with the celibate state.

It is essentially dissatisfaction with the structures, the
training, and the styles of priestly activity which inhibit
the development precisely of those qualities of loving
service for which celibacy exists, and makes a cruel and
sick joke out of the great gift a person makes of himself
when he chooses celibacy. To paraphrase Chesterton
somewhat, it is not that celibacy has been tried and found
wanting, but that structures and training which would
facilitate the flowering of celibate love have been found
hard and not tried. Only the most drastic and immediate
reform of the training and the structures of priestly life
and work will change the situation and give clerical
celibacy a chance. If there are not drastic reforms, and
soon, then I very much fear that the western Church is
going to have to lose celibacy before, in some distant
century, it discovers once again its purpose and meaning.

8

The Priest and Women

WE ACKNOWLEDGE that celibacy is often an excuse and a defense against any fully human relationship. The celibate decision, in this instance, is not a gift made by a mature person but a self-deceiving, self-defeating, self-protecting escape of an immature one. It is an act which is relatively easy to make because it is made by those who are not sure of their own sex role and whose attitude toward women is that of the perennial adolescent. That is to say, a woman becomes a thing, an object, a pleasure, and not a person. We need only to attend certain clerical bull sessions and listen with some sensitivity to realize that many priests are highly exploitative in their attitudes toward women, and are afraid to let some of the elements that are to be found in everyone's personality develop.

Their loud locker room masculinity is only a cover-up for their own fear of women and feeling of sexual inadequacies. We must all of us acknowledge that we are in some fashion or other afraid of women. Honesty further compels us to admit, I think, that we realize at least dimly that most women know that we are frightened by them, and are not quite sure how to cope with this fear.

Eugene Kennedy has often said the greatest problem in the Church is homosexuality rather than heterosexuality. By this he does not mean that there is widespread overt homosexuality in the priestly or religious life (there is not), but rather that the priesthood is a refuge for some men who have never developed the ability to have an honest and authentic relationship with anyone (of either sex). In the clergy they create for themselves a position in which they are secure from healthy human affection, and can nevertheless exercise dominance over others to reassure themselves of their own masculinity. You can take it almost as a rule of thumb that he who is the loudest in his locker room maleness and most insistent on the virtues of all-male camaraderie (usually of the loud or corny variety) is the one who is most insecure in his own maleness and most incapable of honest human relationships. Father Kennedy also adds that he suspects that a good number of those clergy who seem most eager to marry in the present celibacy debate (including some of those who write about it) are extremely dubious about their own masculinity, and want (or "need") a wife so that she will reassure them that they are really men.

The question therefore arises, Ought priests to love women? The answer to this question is so obvious that it almost need not be made. Women are people; priests must love people; therefore, priests must love women. There is no escaping the requirement that a priest's deep, tender, honest human love is not to be limited to half the human race. Nor is there any way of escaping the fact that this love will be a sexual love since humans are sexual creatures, and all relations among human beings whether within their own sex or across sexual lines are inevitably profoundly sexual relationships. Thus, must the priest have sexual love for women? The only answer is that if he is to be a human being there is no escape from it.

Note well, I said sexual, not genital. The failure to make this distinction is one of the grave weaknesses of much of contemporary Catholic discussion of the subject. That every human relationship is colored by sex does not at all mean that every human relationship is pre-ordained to become genital. Modern psychology teaches that man is a sexual animal, and it also teaches us, if we are willing to listen to it, that there are many healthy varieties of sexual behavior which are not at all inevitably and necessarily genital. Friendship within one's own sex or across sexual lines with others can be profoundly in-fluenced by sex, be extremely healthy, and at the same time involve only the very remote possibility of sexual intercourse.

We immediately react, of course, by recalling our seminary experience and training which warned us of the dangers of emotional involvement with women. It assured us that if we have love—much less sexual love—for the female half of the human race, we will shortly lose our celibacy, be swept away with passion, and be headed with inevitable logic toward the marriage bed.

To this form of spirituality, we must reply that such gonadic determinism out-Freuds Freud to an almost unbelievable extent.

Seminary spiritual training is a strange place to find the manifestation of the "low tradition" of understanding of human love. According to this tradition, there is only one kind of possible love between man and woman— marital love—and only one kind of love possible between men and other men, and that is homosexual love. There is, of course, a "high tradition," a tradition which antedates Christianity but which was certainly reinforced by Christianity. That tradition sees human love as a vastly pluralistic phenomenon and admits the possibility of a wide variety of healthy relations between the sexes and within the same sex beside that which is manifested in genital sexuality.

Christianity has always recognized the possibility of sexual relationships which are not marital or genital. The

Lord's relationships, which I mentioned before, with Lazarus and his sisters, with John the Evangelist, with Mary Magdalene, the various relationships between the saints, Clara and Francis of Assisi, Francis of Sales and Louise Marillac, are but a few examples that come readily to mind. All of these establish that Christianity has consistently endorsed the high tradition. But we have yet to overcome the influences of the low tradition with its knowing wink, its dirty laugh, and its vulgar sneer. Curiously enough, most of the critics of ecclesiastical celibacy and its most ardent defenders—the spiritual directors of our seminary past—shared this tradition.

If we permit ourselves to love women, will we be swept away by passion? We will, of course, if we are a blob, merely an aggregation of discrete personality variables, if we are not in full possession of ourselves. If we are basically immature personalities, the advice of the seminary spiritual directors was right. We should not trust ourselves in human love either of men or of women because we are not prepared to cope with it. But if we are reasonably mature adults in reasonable possession of our own personalities, then not only can we love others, be they men or women, but we must. We are driven to do so by the inevitable thrust and force of our basic human personality, and if we try not to, we will succeed simply in destroying ourselves. Is there a danger of being swept away by passion? One supposes there is, but there is a

danger in getting up out of bed in the morning or cross-
ing the street or going out of our house. If we are to
reject every kind of human behavior because there is
danger attached to it, then it is very much to be feared
that we will spend the rest of our lives in the safety of
our beds with the horrendous realization that that is
where most people die.

If priests are mature and adult human beings, not only
may they have love—fully human and sexual love, though
not genital—for women, but they really have no choice
in the matter. This is the inevitable thrust of the mature
human personality to love others regardless of their sex.
The question remains, however, as to what in practice
our behavior with women really is.

A couple of years ago at one of the first group discussion retreats in which I participated, a talk was given by
a layman who raised the question of the behavior of
priests toward women, and raised it in a charitable but
very blunt and outspoken fashion. It was the end of the
possibility of introducing any other subject on the retreat.
The layman had obviously touched a sensitive nerve, and
had released a flow of anxiety and fear that had been
dammed up inside of most of us for all our lives as
priests. Few if any of us had really discussed the subject
before, and the opportunity to discuss it openly without
fear was one simply not to be passed up.

What the gentlemen had said was something that I

think all of us deep down in our subconscious or unconscious had feared even though we had hidden ourselves behind a slick, smooth, and witty veneer. Most women find that our approach of supermasculinity makes us awkward, rude, boorish, and ill-mannered. We are frightened by them and have exploitative, domineering attitudes toward them. Our uncomfortableness and our awkwardness are designed to keep them at a distance. Our fears and confusions and ambiguities in our relationships with women must be straightened out, or we make utter fools of ourselves and leave most sensitive women wondering at the end of their conversations with us whether we will now go back to the rectory and, like other late adolescent males, reassure ourselves of our masculinity by reading the latest issue of *Playboy.*

I do not pretend even vaguely to understand what might be the solution to this problem. Many of us acquired from our family background highly rigid and inflexible Jansenistic attitudes toward sex, and at least some of us inherited from our fathers their fear of our mothers. Our experience in high school and in the seminary merely reinforced our tendency to objectify women, to turn them either into idols to be placed on a pedestal or objects of pleasure to be exploited. The fact that we got close neither to the goddess nor the prostitute merely reinforced our semiconscious fantasies. Only through some fortunate chance did we experience any relationships

with women (even with our own sisters) which enabled
us to come to see that women were persons like we were,
and that whatever physical and psychological differences
existed, the common humanity far transcended these
differences. Given the general American confusion about
sex role, such a hang-up in uncertainty over our own
masculinity is not an unexpected phenomenon. Nor is it
limited to the celibates. And it is not cured by marriage.
But our training and our lives have reinforced the ob-
scurity and uncertainty we feel about our sex role and
have prevented us from developing the styles of protective behaviors which most American males have managed
to put together in their relationships with women.

I am not altogether sure that for many of us the problem is even soluble. The changes in seminary training
currently taking place may well eliminate it in another
generation, though the eager immaturity with which so
many seminarians approach young women makes me
wonder whether even a generation is going to suffice to
root out the effects of many long years of Manicheanism.

It is possible that individuals among us can make great
progress by acknowledging to ourselves how serious this
problem is and how important it is that we begin to grow
toward a solution. Until such an acknowledgment is
made, it seems to me that progress is practically impossible, and I suspect that the resistance to such an acknowledgment is going to be very strong.

On occasions it has occurred to me that an interesting possibility would be group therapy sessions for interested clergy, sessions which would be presided over by a trained, competent therapist who was also a woman. Such sessions might be extremely helpful for many of us in eliminating broad areas of immaturity from our life. The fact that the therapist was a woman might enable us in a secure and controlled environment to begin to understand what a meaningful relationship with a member of the opposite sex might be like. This is only a passing fancy that periodically occurs to me, though I must confess that from the social scientific point of view I would be extremely interested in seeing what results would come from such an experiment.

There is another and more difficult and obscure question which must be asked. We have established, I think, that priests must have a mature, warm, human love for the women among their people as well as for the men. We must ask now whether it is possible for a celibate to have an even deeper relationship with a member of the opposite sex. Is intimate love possible for a celibate? My impression is that we are approaching a period in the Church when this very delicate and difficult question is going to demand an answer and we would only be deceiving ourselves if we refuse to face the question.

The most balanced response to this issue is the one that

Father Eugene Kennedy* has taken and, if I understand his position, it includes the following elements:

a) Intimate friendships are possible for celibates which, far from leading inevitably to the marriage bed, can confirm one more deeply in one's own celibate position.

b) Such relationships are only for the reasonably mature personality. There is so much power and strength in them that the immature ought not fool around with them because they are incapable of such friendships.

c) This kind of intimate sexual friendship cannot be sought. It is not an end that one pursues in itself. It is "given." It is something that happens for some people and does not happen for others, and any conscious attempt to seek it out will be self-defeating or disastrous and would in any case be a sign of immaturity.

d) If such a love is given, it is given for the service of the Church and not even principally for the joy and the happiness of the people involved. Therefore, if it does not contribute to a deepening and enriching of the service of the Church, it is not of the Spirit of God, and has no place in the life of a celibate.

e) The love of which we are speaking is increasingly being manifested in the Church, and it may well represent

* Cf. Eugene Kennedy, M.M., *Fashion Me A People*, Sheed & Ward, New York, 1967.

the special inspiration of the Spirit as he prepares mankind for a major breakthrough in human understanding, a breakthrough which will underline not only in theory but in widespread practice the fact that profound intimate love can exist in a wide variety of ways among mankind and need not be limited to the marital relationship.

f) The kinds of intimate friendship described ought not to be confused with the immature and exploitative crushes of some of the members of the new breed whose desperate search for "experience" is but a renewed manifestation of adolescence and of their own victimization by what Father Kennedy calls "the male mystique."

I submit this as my summary of Father Kennedy's position without necessarily endorsing it but I must make the following comments:

a) The danger of self-deception is very great, and there is so much immaturity and instability and ambiguity among us that I suspect that even if Father Kennedy is right, the number of such relationships that are possible must be very limited.

b) We do not have the theoretical rhetoric or the practical organizational structure to cope with such relationships. This is not to say that they cannot exist but simply that they can be readily misunderstood, even indeed by

the people involved in them. It will be a long time before
the Church as an organization is able to modify its understanding and reorganize its institutions so that such
loves become possible without a great deal of difficulty
and despite a great many obstacles.

c) Nevertheless, I have seen enough cases of what apparently is the kind of love that Father Kennedy describes
to be extremely wary of easy refutations of his position. I,
for one, am not about to argue with the Holy Spirit, and if
this is the way he is beginning to operate in our world
and in our Church, then there are some theoretical reasons to suspect that such operation is perfectly consistent
with his previous operation and some practical reasons to
further suspect that if indeed this be the direction of the
Spirit, it will lead to a tremendous enrichment of the life
of the Church and the life of the whole human race.

As I have thought about Father Kennedy's position
and as I have heard others discuss it, I've found myself
wondering on occasion if it is not possible that the kind
of profound, noble, and beautiful human love of which
he and others are speaking may not have existed frequently in the Church and indeed may not exist even
relatively frequently today. I am not sure, and as a sociologist I'm not going to make judgments in the absence of
data, but if Father Kennedy is right, then I wonder
whether the manifestation of love, intimate and yet celi-

bate, of which he speaks has been limited to our own time. Is it not possible it may have existed often before but that we know nothing about it because there did not exist the rhetoric that was able to describe it or an ecclesiastical structure that was able to cope with it? These relationships, some of them obviously much healthier than others, may have existed for a long time and have for an equally long time represented the finger of God, a finger which only now is beginning to pull back the veil. But these are speculations, and we must admit that only the future will reveal to us the full truth.

I think we would be well-advised to be extremely skeptical about any case where such love is claimed—either in our lives or in the lives of others. But I would argue that we ought to keep an open mind on the theoretical possibility of such relationships both because of the past history of the Church and the wisdom of modern psychology. Unfortunately, it is difficult for us to keep our minds open on any subject, since we were trained to believe that there were very few questions to which there were not clear and simple answers—arrived at long ago.

In conclusion, priests, like most other people, have many kinks, many hang-ups, many distortions in their personalities, but the one that can be most damaging is self-deception. On the subject which we have discussed in the last two chapters a healthy adult reaction would be to say, "Yes, of course I do have those kinds of problems and I can with effort and diligence resolve at least some of them." The immature adolescent reaction would be to say, "Not for me; celibacy and women, they haven't been any problem for me at all." I would suggest anyone who thinks this way is separating himself from the lot of man and in effect denying his membership in the human race, a race membership which is made considerably more pleasant, as well as considerably more difficult, by the fact that it has two sexes instead of just one.

9

Learning in the Life of the Priest

It is difficult to speak to most American priests about the need for learning. Even though most of us admit that we are not reading enough, we still do not take study very seriously, and have acute guilt feelings about any time we spend away from our "work" reading and thinking. We are, more recently at least, given to the American addiction for "taking courses," but almost always we justify such activity in terms of its practical utility. Taking a course on liturgy will help us better to instruct our people. Taking a course in scripture will help us to give better sermons. Taking a course in psychology will help us to be better counselors. I would be the last one in the world to criticize better sermons and better counseling and better liturgy. We need more rather than less of these phe-

123

nomena. But I would like to submit that something quite different from the taking-a-course mentality is needed in the contemporary priesthood.

Unfortunately, it frequently seems that many clergy do not even have the intellectual categories to cope with this need. When one speaks to them about the need for theory, they look at one with the same mystification that Engine Charlie Wilson betrayed when he referred to basic research as curiosity about what makes grass green and that Ronald Reagan manifested when he affirmed that he did not think that the people of California were interested in subsidizing intellectual curiosity. The American clergy are, by and large, men of action, not men of reflection; doers, and not dreamers or thinkers. Theorizing may be fine in its place but theory has few practical implications in the daily work of the priest, and so he has little time for it. As Father George Florowski says of tradition, it is not a question of theory or no theory, but of good theory or bad theory. By theory I mean the basic assumptions, often barely above the threshold of consciousness, which underlie our behavior and our attitudes. We all have, I suspect, very detailed theories about what the Church is, about what man is, about what human life is, and about what the priesthood is. Unfortunately, since we never make these theories explicit, we rarely, if ever, are able to reexamine and reevaluate them, much less change them. Our theory, on which all our practical behavior is based, therefore, is fixed and unchanging. Such fixed and unchanging theory may be harmless in a priest in an era of great stability in the Church, but in our present time of dynamic confusion the priest whose theoretical assumptions are rooted in the clichés of the past is simply not going to be able to deal with the problems of the present. As Lord Keynes remarked, in the long run there is nothing more practical than good theory.

To be a man of hope the priest must be a man of vision and must be able to see a vision, and to constantly renew it the priest must be a man of wisdom. But wisdom is not acquired automatically or by accident. Wisdom is the result of thought and of theorizing. If the priest is not intellectually curious, he does not think; if he is not constantly refining and reforming his theories, it is terribly difficult to see how he can keep his vision alive and growing. Under such circumstances it would be unrealistic to expect him to be a man of hope, particularly in a time when the Church is going through great and traumatic changes.

At the root of our problem is the persistence of anti-intellectualism in the American Church. This anti-intellectualism is understandable in terms of the history and sociology of immigrant groups trying to adjust to the New World. It is not that we did not value ideas; it was simply that we had no time for them. We were too busy struggling for survival to become very self-conscious about what we were doing. We were able to accomplish so much with so little pure thought that we have now managed to deceive ourselves that one can continue and move ahead in American society doing much and thinking little.

One of the classic examples of this is the parochial school. We came to the United States, many of us at least, from countries where the public school system was officially a means for proselytizing Catholic children. In this country we discovered that the public schools tended to be vaguely Protestant in their orientation. We, therefore, began to build our own schools to preserve and deepen the faith of our children. However, the world changed and education changed. Public schools became quite neutral and stopped being anti-Catholic in even the remotest way.

Research began to demonstrate that there was no substantial proselytizing among Catholics in public schools, and that the vast majority of public school Catholics remained practicing Catholics in adult life. Some of them even became priests and bishops. Nonetheless, we continued to build our schools without bothering to rethink the theory on which such construction was based. Then the critics of Catholic education appeared on the scene with little more in the way of empirical data to justify their criticisms than we had theoretical foundations to justify the existence of the schools. When they began to suggest that Catholic schools were not the "answer" (it was never quite clear what the question is for which parochial schools are not the answer), we suddenly found ourselves without any theoretical grounds on which to base our reaction to criticism. The result has been an incredible collapse of morale within Catholic educational circles, almost as though many Catholic teachers and administrators have feared all along that the critics were right even before the criticism started. The only justifications for Catholic schools were ad hoc ones, and the critics denied the relevancy of the ad hoc justifications. It has seemed to many Catholics, especially those within the educational system, that the schools have had it.

At this point I do not wish to enter in the controversy over the continuation of Catholic schools. I simply want to point out that if at some stage in our frantic construction of a separate Catholic school system we had paused to think through in depth the rationale behind such a school system (in terms that go beyond mere citations from ecclesiastical documents), we would not find ourselves in a situation where every meeting of Catholic educators turns into a wake. The real problem in Catholic education today is not so much public disaffection, but rather the collapse of morale within the system, a collapse which, in my judgment, is based entirely on the lack of sound theory.

Again I think that perhaps the basic weakness of the

great Catholic Action movements which began in Chicago is that the men that founded them and have administered them have been almost incredibly skillful at the arts of diplomacy and politics but have never really bothered to provide solid theoretical bases for what they have been doing, and so were caught completely unprepared by the dramatic changes of the Vatican Council. One magnificent, ideological insight has sustained organizations like Cana and the Christian Family Movement for a quarter of a century; but when that insight has lost its thrust, Cana and the Christian Family Movement and other organizations begin to flail around looking for new theories and discovering that none are to be had.

The trouble is that we American Catholics have so little self-consciousness. Even in our best universities there is practically no study of either the history or the sociology of the American Church—though our historical tradition is an astonishingly impressive one. The voices of Carroll, England, Gibbons, Ireland, and Spalding have extremely relevant things to say for our time. The American tendency (not limited to the Catholics) is to dash into the future with little concern for the past from which we come or even for the precise nature of the present in which we stand.

Even though we may be nice to him personally, we have precious little respect either for the scholar or for his scholarship. We demonstrate this by our attitude toward research. We approach the research scholar and the research organization as though research were a gigantic computer into which we could feed a certain number of questions and which would feed back the "answers," or which would at least tell us what questions we should be asking. We approach men of research and say, "Come and study us and tell us what to do," without ever bothering to discover whether such an attitude betrays any understanding of what research is or what the scholar does. Our attitude is, "I haven't got time to study the problems of the research enterprise and I really haven't got time to listen to you speak to me of your difficulties. I just want to know how to do it and I must know how as quickly as possible."

We want practical answers, and we want them soon, and are not terribly interested either in the nature of research or its limitations or in attempts to find the underlying theoretical explanation which must be achieved before solid practical answers are remotely possible.

This obsession of Americans with gimmicks, panaceas, and simple how-to-do-it instructions leaves no room for concern about long-range vision. Unfortunately, if we are not concerned about long-range vision, the gimmicks we randomly and indiscriminately seize upon will be of no help to us, and the more compulsive we are about trying something new, the more chaotic and confused our situation will become. We are eager, so pathetically eager, to grab for the short-run, the simple answer, the new gimmick, the latest technique, the newest party line, whether it be the missal, or salvation history, or group dynamics, or sensitivity training, or whatever bright new schemes flash across the horizon. But we have no time either to fashion a broad and general vision of what we are about, or to thoroughly examine an innovation to determine whether it can be integrated into such a vision. Our training, our cultural background, and our intellectual posture make it extremely difficult for us to think.

Under such circumstances, journalists replace scholars. The journalists, whatever their merits, have little tolerance for complexity and almost no ability to devise anything beyond the most simpleminded kinds of theory. If I might speak personally of my own experience for a moment, my colleagues and I spent three years and a quarter of a million dollars in an extraordinarily careful and detailed study of the effects of Catholic education. While the study has been received very favorably by our non-Catholic colleagues in the social sciences, it has been treated with precious little respect in the Catholic press, with the right-wing being critical because it is not a complete exoneration of Catholic schools and the left-wing being equally critical because it is not a complete damnation of Catholic schools. The report is damned as being mired in qualifications, which means that reality is much more complicated than the critics of the report would like to concede. If you cannot give a clear yes or no answer, not only is your work seen as having little value, but you are judged as being immoral for having sold out to the other side, and this, of course, makes life a little difficult when both sides think you have sold out to the opposite side.

There are several series of negative effects of this lack of authentic intellectual concerns and respect for scholarship. First of all, the take-a-course mentality may actually do more harm than good. A little learning is a very dangerous thing indeed, and the cleric who has simplistic and inadequate training in psychological counseling or in group dynamic techniques is anything but harmless. He has become a positive menace. Similarly, someone who has learned the jargon of salvation history, catechetics, or the new scripture studies, and has confused this ability to manipulate the jargon with wisdom, is not only frequently an insufferable bore; he is also quite capable of confusing the People of God who are already confused enough. Either learning is an important thing, and must be pursued seriously and for its own sake, or it is unimportant, and we should not waste time with it. A half-hearted approach to learning which views it not as a state of mind and an orientation toward reality but as a purveyor of simple answers and interesting new gimmicks is an even more harmful form of clerical anti-intellectualism than that which refuses to concede learning any relevance at all.

Secondly, because the Church in the United States is so disinterested in theory and in learning, it is difficult for a priest who is concerned about theoretical questions to get scholarly training, and this despite the injunctions of Papal and Conciliar documents on the importance of giving specialized training to priest-scholars. He who wants scholarly training must be prepared to fit it in with full- or part-time parish work because only parish work is taken to justify priestly existence. He who attempts to build up the People of God through his scholarship and through his theorizing is viewed as a slacker who has somehow or other managed to arrange a deal for himself to escape from the frontline trenches, which is to say to escape, if possible, from hearing confessions every Saturday afternoon and evening. It never occurs to the critics that the scholar might be the one to raise the question whether the Saturday approach to confession is at all a valid one in the present age.

But if we do not have scholars to ask deep and probing questions, then we will simply keep on doing what we have always done long after it has ceased to be relevant, and we will not have scholars unless we are willing to give them the time and the freedom to pursue their scholarship. We will not do this unless we have among the body of the clergy a profound respect for scholarship. (I might add that after this respect there also probably ought to come a profound skepticism of some of the things that scholars do, but one cannot have a legitimate skepticism about scholarship until one first of all comes to know and respect scholarship for what it is.)

Thirdly, because we have no basic curiosity beyond the

pragmatic, we find ourselves equipped with little flexibility or playfulness or imagination in approaching problems; yet successful and creative innovation can only come when the innovator can be flexible and playful in his speculations. We are, therefore, little willing to change some proved methods which are not really proved or to ponder playfully the possibilities of a wide variety of other methods. It matters not whether we call ourselves liberals or conservatives because the liberal in American Catholicism tends to be more dogmatic and inflexible than the conservative. The prophets and charismatic leaders of one generation of the Negro apostolate or Catholic Action activities become the close-minded tyrants of another generation. The process will continue inevitably until we can break the vicious circle of narrowness, inflexibility, and refusal to think, to dream, and to imagine.

Narrowness and anti-intellectualism, opinionated stubbornness, and the absence of respect for theory and scholarship and learning are hardly the stuff which produce visions, nor are they the stuff out of which prophets are made, nor are they what the Church needs in a time of ambiguity, crisis, and pilgrimage. A pilgrimage must be searching and experimental. He who leads the pilgrimage, even though he has a mighty vision of the direction in which he is going, must be constantly ready to play it by ear, to experiment, but to experiment within the context of his understanding of the direction in which the experiment should go. Hence, *a priori* answers or magisterial simplicity will not work; nor will stubbornness and arrogance. Yet on the intellectual level there is a strong temptation for American priests to think that they either have all the answers or they know where the answers can be acquired, and that the answers are, in the final analysis, simple and clear ones.

Nor is this the weakness merely of the old clergy; the personalist refusal of the young to have any answers at all is in itself the most dogmatic of answers. Their refusal to admit that there may be anything in the wisdom of the past that can be a basis for organic growth in the present is a narrow anti-intellectualism as objectionable as any other brand of anti-intellectualism to be observed in American Catholicism.

You will note that I have not spoken explicitly about the reading of books or magazines. I presume that any priest who is at all interested in the priesthood becomes an avid reader. I am arguing rather that reading simply is not enough, that it must be linked with a basic, underlying orientation of intellectual curiosity and respect for ideas and theories. I will contend the American clergy desperately needs respect for learning and ideas and to a considerable extent does not have it. Can we get it? Yes, we can. How? For this question I refuse to attempt a simple answer.

10

The Priest
and Professional
Standards

THE WORD PROFESSIONAL can be used in two senses. It can mean the man who has the professional manner, who is dispassionate and reserved, who is interested only in your right eye, or your income tax, or your wisdom tooth, or your life insurance, and not in you as a person; he is a man who selects out one segment of your life and becomes a specialist in it. This is not the sense in which I am using professional in the present chapter. If this sort of smooth, glib professionalism has made any inroads at all in the clergy, then I think one of the first things we must do in the renewal of the priesthood is to root it out. I am not sure that the specialist lawyer or doctor is, in the long run, an asset to the medical or legal profession, but his counterpart certainly is not an asset to the priesthood.

We already have more than enough careerists in our numbers.

I use *professional* as applying to a man who works principally with his mind and imagination, who has highly specialized skills which he has developed through long training, and who operates not so much because of external constraint or even simply for financial gains but out of interiorized dedication to the standards of the work he is doing. Whether a priest is, in fact, a professional in this sense of the word may be an open question. We ought to be; but a training which warned us against the dangers of thinking for ourselves, hinted broadly that most of the things we were learning in the seminary would be worthless after ordination, subjected our lives to constant external restraint and constraint and prevented us from interiorizing motivations, hardly prepared us for professionalization. Herein, of course, is the precise problem which we must face. Society expects us to be professionals. If we are to do our work well as priests, we must have professional standards, and yet we were trained in a fashion which strongly inhibits the development of professionalism.

But there are at least several aspects of professional behavior which we might ponder.

The professional has pride in his work. What he does, he does well not merely because he is forced to do so, not merely because his income depends on it, but because his respect for his work compels him to set high standards in his work. If we are to behave as professionals, then we must have high standards in our work too. What we do, we must do well. It is better that in some matters we do nothing rather than do it poorly. Thus, our parochial liturgies, the very core of the Eucharistic community over which we preside, must be of the highest quality or there is no reason to expect that anything else we do will have high quality. We ought to remark in passing that the parking problem is not, after all, the most serious issue facing the Church, and Sunday liturgies which are organized around the needs of the parking problem or the need of having priests in the rectory basement counting money are in fact a disgrace and a perversion of the true meaning of the liturgy.

There are few of us who would argue that our preaching standards are such to justify any claim to professionalism. The laity's complaints about preaching are increasingly vocal, and as we become more and more involved in the new Church, we must be prepared to expect that criticism of our impoverished and mediocre speaking abilities is going to be made more and more to our faces. Our lay people are going to insist that we either improve our preaching or quietly step aside for those who do know how to preach. It is no good to fall back on the simple explanation that our homiletics training in the seminary was usually abominable. Abominable, of course, it was.

But we are literate; we are equipped with imaginations; we presumably can put a subject and a predicate together.

Our poor preaching is not based on physical incapacities or even on the absence of training but on the fact that a) we have not so resolved our own internal emotional problems as to be even relatively at ease in front of a congregation, and b) our learning and our imaginations have become so stagnant that we really do not have anything to say to people. Hence, we turn to the clichés and the truisms that we may have heard ourselves when we were sitting on the other side of the communion rail. I would suggest that sometime when you are on vacation you attend a parish Mass anywhere in the country and listen to the sermon. See what it is like to be on the other side of the rail once again. In most instances it will be an extraordinarily painful experience.

Our work of administering and organizing the parish also must be done with professional elegance. Because we can get away with shoddy work does not mean that it is not shoddy or that people do not realize that it is shoddy. Today it simply means that the respect of the Catholic laity for their clergy is still such that they will not tell Father to his face that he is an incompetent bungler who has never learned even the basic elements of planning and organizing and executing which everyone in the world of business and profession has to learn at the beginning of his career. We can respond that in the seminary we were given no opportunity to organize our own lives or to administer anything on our own initiative and responsibility, that even in the parishes we are often errand boys between pastor and people. This all may be very true, but it does not excuse us from seriousness in the organizational activity in which we become involved.

It is to be presumed, of course, that our long years of education have enabled us to write, but one need only examine parish bulletins (and one need not limit this examination merely to the atrocious examples that turn up in the columns of the *National Catholic Reporter*) to discover that many of us are not too literate, that our styles are either simplemindedly pious or pompously arrogant. We have never gone through the trouble of learning how to put together a decent English sentence.

Let me note here that far more diocesan priests are capable of serious literary effort than actually engage in it. I count this a first-rate tragedy because I would suspect, for example, that there may be as many as a hundred priests in the Archdiocese of Chicago who are capable of turning out several excellent articles or one good book every few years. Their failure to do so deprives the Church of powerful witnesses. It takes courage to begin to write, I suppose, especially since there are so many of our colleagues in the priesthood who are ready to begin shooting at us as soon as we dare step out of the

ranks and begin to express ourselves on the printed page.
In our day it takes less courage because there is more
respect and value for serious writing now than there was
ten or fifteen or twenty years ago. But I would like to note
that I think the opposition and criticism are greatly ex-
aggerated. Any priest who begins to write seriously would
discover that he is going to get far more support from his
colleagues than he will opposition. But if we are going to
write, let us write well, or let us not bother to write at all.

Our teaching must be professional. Unless we have
kept up with the developments in catechetics influenced
by educational psychology, unless we have thoroughly
read not only the documents of the Vatican Council but
some of the vast literature of interpretation that has
grown up around the Council, I fail to see how we can
enter a classroom, inquiry class, or even preach a sermon
on Sunday morning. It would be like a doctor insisting
that it was unnecessary for him to know anything about
antibiotics, or a psychiatrist insisting there is no reason
in the world why he should read Freud. If we have not
kept up with the literature on the Vatican Council, if we
do not understand clearly the profound nature of the
changes the Council worked in the Church, then it is
difficult for me to see how we can consider ourselves anything but a menace to the Church.

Finally, if we are going to counsel, let us counsel pro-
fessionally. Let us strive to understand as clearly and as

explicitly as possible the theory and methods of counseling and not assume that our own experience or our own innate wisdom tells us more about how counseling ought to be done than can those who are experts at it. The priest who views the counseling session as nothing more than a sophisticated way of giving advice and making decisions for other people can hardly be said to have professional standards.

If we are, therefore, to have pride in our work we must keep up with the developments in our profession. In other words, we must read, read constantly, read not merely because it is an escape or a form of relaxation, but read because it is an essential part of our professional development. If we are to be effective priests, we must read a vast variety of books and magazines. For purely pragmatic reasons, if for no other, we cannot afford to let ourselves become isolated from the developments of ideas in the Church. Never again ought we to have the sort of experience of shock, dismay, and disbelief that occurred when the first symposia on the "new" approaches to scripture were presented to our American priests. Anyone who had done minimal reading in the field of bible studies would have been prepared for such symposia, and the reaction throughout the country was unquestioned proof, if we need any, that most priests simply had read about the scriptures, about the word of God, about a primary font of Christian revelation.

The response comes, of course, that we have no time to read, but this is nonsense. We have no time *not* to read if we have any professional self-respect. Reading is as critical in our life as is prayer or work, and to quote one of John Hotchkin's epigrams, "We must not let the urgent interfere with the important; we must not let our work interfere with our leisure." These paradoxes are painfully true. If we do not have the leisure to read, reflect, and think, then our work will become sterile, stagnant, and dry. We will lose ourself in a frenzy of activity and become a machine or a computer, if you will, but not a human being who thinks for himself and decides for himself. To say that we cannot read means that we do not have enough personal security to detach ourselves from the work of the moment and that we view the reality in which we live and work as essentially uncontrollable. It has so captured us that we are not able to escape from it even for a brief period each day to think and study intelligently about it.

If we are professionals, we display professional responsibility and reliability. The great and unspoken secret among the laity is that you really cannot count on most priests to do what they say they will do, much less to do it on time, indeed even to return a phone call. There are all kinds of allowances and apologies made on the basis that Father does so much or Father is so busy or Father is so good, but most laymen do not regard us as being very reliable professionals. Small wonder, of course; we were never permitted during our training and were often not permitted in the parish to act on our own initiative and responsibility. On the contrary, the basic motivation for our activity was fear and constraint. Under such circumstances we never developed enough of a selfhood to be capable of responsible and reliable behavior. But just because we are able to deceive ourselves that we are good administrators and because the laity have thus far left us in our ignorance, it does not follow that we have much time left to recognize the fact that in many ways we are quite unreliable and irresponsible. This irresponsibility, particularly about time and commitments, is especially obvious among some of the new breed who seem to think that punctuality and responsibility interfere with spontaneity, self-fulfillment, and personalism. Their personalism seems to mean respect for their own persons, but hardly for the persons with whom they work and, particularly, for the time of these persons. The laity may understand the reasons why, and they may feel sorry for us because we are not able to be mature enough to be responsible and reliable and punctual, but this does not make our behavior any more professional than it really is.

At the root of our unreliability is the vice of overcommitment, the giving in to the temptation to try to assume that one must do far more than it is possible for him to do. Confusion of zeal with compulsive and pathological activity is a confusion which in itself is irresponsible and immature. The Lord does not expect us to do everything, particularly if in our attempts we do everything poorly. He expects us to do that which is possible for us to do, and to do it well, and the limits of the possible are limits imposed by the possibility of excellence and not of mediocrity.

A professional is eager to work with others within his profession. Close relationships with professional colleagues are not seen as a threat to one's independence or security but rather as an extremely valuable asset in his professional development and in the quality of his service. Among the really good professionals there are no lone-wolves. But for us it is frequently just the opposite. We were trained in suspicion and distrust and have produced a large number of apostolic lone-wolves who cannot co-operate or will not cooperate, and who cannot communicate or receive communication, or who at least will not communicate or receive communication. They cannot give orders or take orders; they cannot integrate their own talents into a collegial relationship; and further they cannot accept the talents of others as an assistance to their own.

This is the function of priestly obedience. Obedience is simply that form of self-discipline and self-focusing which enables us to integrate our talents and abilities. Obedience, like chasity and like poverty, is essentially a func-

obscure their clerical identity but fabricate wild fictional accounts of who and what they are, may temporarily take delight in the deceptions that they are accomplishing; but I rather suspect that they fool fewer people than they think, no matter how successful they are at fooling themselves.

In conclusion, the professional model is a difficult one or us to imitate. Clearly we must be far more professional an we have been, but we cannot be more professional til at least we have begun to take seriously the con- t of the priest as an honest, mature, responsible, re- le professional.

tional virtue. Its function is to produce a smoothly operating and cooperating professional college of clergy. If our obedience contributes to the development of such a collegial system, then it is a virtue, and if it does not, then it is a vice. Priestly obedience which is praiseworthy must be based on interiorized commitment to cooperation rather than externalized conformity to rules. Obedience, therefore, is one of the forces which makes professional cooperation possible.

Even among professional colleagues in law or medicine the virtue of obedience is required, but it is obedience which represents a commitment to a joint decision rather than the passive acceptance of an order from on high. This obedience is much more difficult and requires much higher professional standards than does the obedience of external conformity.

But cooperation with others is not easy for us unless we are able to trust others. Our rectories are often filled with such suspicion and distrust that even civil communication is impossible, much less a high level of professional cooperation which ought to be expected among priests. We keep coming back to the same root problem. Professional cooperation and the integration of our own talents into the professional college require far more maturity than many of us are able to muster. We hide behind our frightened sense of independence or our injured sense of self-pity. We even generate conflicts with our brother priests as a pretext for not having to cooperate with them. We deceive ourselves that the whole world is against us when the real truth is that we are not brave enough or mature enough or conscious enough of ourselves to even begin to trust others, much less trust them to the extent of working closely with them.

Yet another professional standard is that which makes a professional eager to take initiative and responsibility and to act on his own. The true professional sees what needs to be done in a situation and does it without waiting to be told or without even waiting until every last detail of the meaning of his role is resolved. One reason why the authoritarianism of the pastor-curate relationships survived so long is that, for all their complaints, many curates liked it that way. They did not have to think for themselves or act for themselves; they merely had to do what they were told. Nor did they need take any responsibility. If a project failed, if a work was undone, if a need was unmet, they were surely not to blame. It was the pastor's fault. What a marvelous scapegoat the pastor has been! For the new breed the scapegoat for inactivity is a bit different. They no longer blame the pastor; they now blame the lack of clarity about the priestly role. As we have seen, there are increasing numbers of young clerics who do little, if anything, save long for the inner city "where the action is," on the pretext that they do not know what to do. This does not show

much professional initiative, but then they a
fessionals.

The last professional standard I wish to m
standard of honesty. Lawyers, doctors, or r
ars, at least if they are good ones, tell only t
do not run away from complexity, uncerta
culty. They do not try to make things
they are not, nor do they pretend to h
when answers are not available. They d
hide things from their colleagues or tl
play the game straight or they do not p
is not necessarily crude, blunt, offen
(as some new breeders would like u
rather urbane and tactful and diplo
mature personality does not permit
into thinking that rudeness is the
neither does it permit the decepti
can fool people over the long h
evasions.

The vague and even distorte
some parishes receive, for fear tl
giving if they knew how good
is bound to be unsuccessful in
Most of our more astute p
assume that the pastor is r
financial report until the co
Finally, those new breed cle

11

The Priest and the Spiritual Life

ALL THE MATERIAL covered in the previous chapters has to do with the spiritual life of the priest, with his sanctification, and with his growth in virtue and holiness. I cannot accept that definition of the spiritual life which excludes concerns about love and hope, maturity and vision, professional standards and intellectual seriousness from the domain of the development of priestly virtue. The rhetoric that I have used in the other chapters is not, I will admit, the rhetoric of traditional spiritual writers, but the rhetoric of the spirituality we absorbed in the seminary is simply not yet able to cope with the full dimensions of holiness required for a priest in the modern world. We cannot be men of God and we cannot be men in union with God if our concept of spirituality is limited

to prayer and mortification as these words are tradition-
ally understood.

I do not want to be understood as excluding prayer and
mortification from the spiritual life of the priest; they are
obviously and clearly parts of it; but they are parts that
are meaningless if they do not exist in a healthy relationship with the priestly virtues discussed in the other
chapters.

We are not monks, and our spirituality ought to be
neither monkish spirituality nor watered-down modified
versions of monkish spirituality. The precisely regulated
prayer of the monastic discipline is an impossibility for
us, and any attempts to imitate it are bound to be self-
defeating. I will not pretend that the breviary is an asset
to our work, and I will not attempt to defend the breviary
as so many writers on priestly holiness do. I very much
fear that for the overwhelming majority of priests, the
breviary, even in English, is a penance and, beyond that,
a waste of time. We say it out of a sense of obedience
and duty, not because we find it a suitable or adequate
prayer for men who, while they point to a world beyond
the modern world, still must be immersed in that world.

This is not to say that some form of systematic daily
prayer is a bad thing. On the contrary, I think it is an
excellent thing, but the Roman breviary as it now stands
has very few of the elements that ought to be found in
such systematized priestly prayer. A drastic reform ought

to be high on the agenda for those concerned with the renewal of priestly spirituality. As one wise and perceptive bishop said of the Roman breviary, "That fellow David, he was no Christian." Reading, mental prayer, and meditations on the scriptures are as essential today as they were in the beginning of Christianity, but the form in which these prayers and devotions come to us now, that is to say, the familiar black book with the red-edged pages, far from contributing to reading, reflection, and meditation, actually impedes these practices. Unless the regular daily prayer of the priest is renewed, and renewed soon, it is much to be feared that the Roman breviary will fall into the same disuse as it enjoyed in the late Middle Ages.

I would think that we must get much of our spirituality from our work. We have to transcend the work, but still must be rooted in the work and oriented toward it. Our work of leadership, teaching, building the community, loving, hoping—these are the sources of our prayer and our penance and our spiritual growth. Particularly severe, it seems to me, is the penance of fighting self-deception which is the essential barrier to living up to the challenges of our priesthood. Self-knowledge, the struggle for maturity, the courage to face our problems and to seek help in their solution, the strength to act reliably and responsibly and maturely—these may not be the only forms of priestly penance, but I do not think it is an exaggeration to say that in the absence of such forms other kinds of penance are largely meaningless.

There are two particular dimensions of what I suppose we might call a traditional spiritual life upon which I would like to comment: contemplation and poverty.

By contemplation I do not mean merely contemplative or reflective prayer. Obviously, we must have this, but reflection, contemplation, mental prayer—call it what we will—is not likely to happen unless there is a contemplative strain that runs through our whole personality; unless, to use existentialist terms, there is a contemplative modality about our being in the world. We must have about us the ability to pull out of daily action and become conscious of our oneness with all creation. Oneness occurs in our very act of perception by which we take all things that we perceive into us; oneness is reinforced by the language and the culture which we share with others; oneness reaches its summation in our love and hope and our trust when we relate to others—the twig, the snow-flake, the street light, the sound of an elevated train, the laughter of a teen-ager, the warmth of an early spring. We must be able to take the time to be transported by these delights out of our own narrowness and self-suffi-ciency and away from the trivial demands of the present moment into a great sense of unity of the being of which we are a part, or we will not be able to pray.

Further, we must be able to give ourselves over unreservedly and with neither guilt nor distraction to the joys of friendship and love, or we will not be able to pray to the God who is our friend and our lover. We must permit ourselves the luxury of dreaming, of thinking, of reflecting, of playful speculative fantasies, of pausing and doing simply nothing, or else we will not be able to pray (and we can only agree with Gilbert Chesterton in his evaluation of the profound advantages of doing nothing). We must permit ourselves the relief of a few moments of quiet and solitude without rushing to the radio or the television or the telephone or dashing down the corridor to another priest's room in order to distract ourselves from the awful experience of being alone, or else we will not be able to pray.

Contemplative prayer does not exist by itself. It must exist in the context of a contemplative personality, or it will not take place. Our spiritual directors at the seminary never seemed to understand this. They thought that by insisting day in and day out on the need for mental prayer, they would develop habits of prayer in us independently of any other dimensions of our personality. They did not understand that the system of personality development which does not take into account the needs for developing the contemplative dimensions of the human personality will be unable to train young men in the habit of prayer. We do not contemplate, we do not reflect, we do not meditate because we do not know how, because our personality is incapable of coping with solitude, quiet, dreams, and the stunted mystical tendencies which are within all of us.

The fear of reflection, quiet, solitude is the fear of the weak and the compulsive personality. Only the strong can permit life to stop for a few minutes so that they are able to contemplate. In the final analysis if we are not strong enough to be contemplative, then it is dubious that we are strong enough to be priests.

While they are not absolutely essential for the development of contemplative personality, art, music, poetry, drama, and fiction actually do help. The reading of novels is not, as we were told in the seminary, generally a waste of time any more than listening to music, visiting museums, or going to the theater need be a waste of time. It might be somewhat of an exaggeration to say that they are prayer, but they surely are an effective predisposition for prayer if we permit them to be. I fail to see how we can be sensitive to the beauty of God and docile to the whisperings of the Spirit if we ignore the God-made or the man-made beauty in the world around us. If we cannot, for example, stand in the busy center of our city at eight o'clock of a spring evening and feel the pulse of the city beating as we observe the wide variety of people that drift by us, then I am not at all sure whether we are really capable of serving those people. In every great city of America we priests must keep in touch with the outstanding art museums, attend local concerts and plays, and pause to appreciate both the ugliness and the beauty of our land.

The second problem which I would like to discuss is the question of priestly poverty. Poverty, first of all, is not an absolute good or an end in itself, just as chastity and obedience are not good in themselves. Our poverty, like everything else, must be functional, for if it does not serve the work of the Church, then there is no place for it in our lives. But it is difficult to know what poverty ought to mean in the life of a contemporary American priest. Ours is an affluent society, which is not to say that everyone is affluent, but that we have the technological and perhaps even the social scientific tools necessary to eliminate poverty. Our society wages, although perhaps somewhat unsuccessfully and unimaginatively, a war against poverty, and our own poverty can hardly be justified by assuming that what we give up somehow or other is going to help the poor and the oppressed and will promote the solution of social problems. It would be nice to think that this were true, and it might have been true at one time in the history of mankind, but today it represents a terribly naive view of social and economic structures.

Nor can our poverty be based on a hatred of material goods. The riches and abundance of this world, from water skis to electric blankets, are good things in themselves, and they were made by God, through human

intervention, for us to enjoy. There is in our day a desperate need for a Christian materialism which puts away the
Jansenism of the past and sees the material goods of this
world for what they are: goods that were meant to serve
us. Jansenism which denies their goodness or their value
is not superior to perverted materialism; it makes them
our masters. As a matter of fact, Jansenism and perverted
materialism may often be simply the different sides of
the same coin.

Nor does it seem to me that our poverty can be based
on the notion of scandal or what others can afford or
what others will think. Scandal, of course, must be considered, and it must be admitted that the clergy have not
at all times, on all occasions, behaved with the utmost
discretion in their use of material goods, but it can hardly
provide us with a definite norm on which to base our own
activities, especially if poverty, like other virtues, is more
of an internal orientation than a response to pressures for
external conformity. What others think about our behavior is something we must judge and take into account
in making our moral decisions, but it cannot provide the
ultimate norm for such decisions.

The norm that is frequently cited—that a priest should
not have anything his parishioners cannot afford—is not
only an extrinsic norm but also would lead to a moral
relativism; in this way poverty would have an entirely
different meaning in one context than it might in another

context. I often find myself puzzled by the priest who says that he cannot play golf because no one in his parish can afford to play golf. Presumably, then, if he moved to a well-to-do parish he could afford to play golf. I would be inclined to suspect such a relativistic approach to poverty; while it may be satisfactory to a given person, it is of no theoretic help at all, and probably will produce a superficial form of poverty. What one's parishioners can afford does provide us with certain norms of fitness and appropriateness, but hardly a useful standard on which to base ultimate decisions.

Furthermore, our poverty surely cannot be founded on a casuistry which tries to provide fixed answers to all questions for all people. I trust I will be excused for the rest of my life from any further discussions on whether Florida vacations are good or bad for priests. This is a silly question, and I think we waste our time in trying to render a judgment on it. Of course Florida vacations are good (and California vacations may be even better), but whether it is a good thing in a particular case depends on whether or not it contributes to the development of the priest's personality and thus to the work of the Church. It is easy to imagine circumstances where it will do so, and other circumstances where it will do exactly the opposite. If a winter vacation in a sunny climate makes a priest a more effective servant of his people, I very much doubt whether the people will take strong exception to it. The kind of cleric whose vacation (and other kinds of material abundance) offends people is the one who is obviously not doing his work, is obviously not presiding over the Eucharistic community in charity. Unfortunately, there are not a few of those still in our numbers.

The critical question about our relationship with material goods is whether our material possessions and comforts contribute to our growth and freedom or rather to our stagnation and enslavement. It would seem to me that it is certainly necessary for us to have some kinds of thoroughly rigorous self-denial in our lives to maintain freedom of movement. Material wealth and possessions have within themselves almost what we might call an innate tendency to make demands on us; the evil is not so much in the material goods as in our weakness in responding to the insistent demands that these goods make. We must therefore develop skills and firmness in response. When material possessions make us happy, they are good; when they become an obsession with us, they are bad. It would seem to be almost an ironclad law of human nature, however, that we can only enjoy them and that they will only make us happy when we impose the limitations of wisdom upon our use of them. But how this is to be done in practice depends, in the present state of our knowledge, almost exclusively on the problems and personality of the individual and the way the Holy Spirit speaks to a priest through his natural intelligence and inclinations and good taste. Good taste, I might remark, can generally be thought to be an excellent norm for priestly poverty. Unfortunately, good taste comes only with maturity and, as we noted before, many of us still have a long way to go before we achieve maturity.

There is also the risk of being mired in possessions, of having accumulated so much material that we lose all our mobility. When it does become necessary to move, we realize how much we have that we never use; it may even occur to us that the acquisitive instinct is stronger than the sexual one and can, on occasion, substitute for it. I wonder, for example, how many of us make use of the tape recorders that almost all of us have. I am surely not opposed to tape recorders, but I am contending that we must resist the urge to be impulse buyers, to latch on to a new gimmick without considering whether we are ever going to use it. We must exclude all tendencies to build monuments to ourselves. The monument-building temptation is a seductive one because we persuade ourselves that the monuments which we have put up are really not for our memory but for the service of our people, without asking ourselves whether the people could be served equally well, and perhaps better, by building something which would be quite conceivably less monumental and more esthetically attractive. If it is true that good taste is a sure sign of maturity, we must admit that some of the churches that we see abroad in the land suggest that not all those who have supervised construction of ecclesiastical plants have been as mature as might be desirable.

Finally, the spirit of poverty among the clergy must include a great deal of generosity—generosity which comes rather close to being the same thing as the previously mentioned avoidance of clutter. Generosity must have about it a prudence and a discretion because we are stewards, and the goods have been entrusted to us, and the Lord expects us to exercise our stewardship intelligently. One of the most impressive characteristics of the American clergy is their generosity; while people may be shocked or scandalized (often pardonably so) by some of the goods and clutter that priests amass, far more often they are impressed and edified by manifestations of priestly generosity. I will not say that poverty is not a problem of the American clergy. How could it help but be a problem in an affluent society like ours? But I do not think it is the most serious problem we face, nor do I believe that it is a problem that will get completely out of hand as long as generosity continues.

Beyond these points the meaning of poverty in an age of affluence is obscure. However, the crucial principle is not obscure. Material goods are good and are meant to be enjoyed. They are meant to make us happy, yet we can misuse them and degrade them by twisting them into masters that they are not designed to be but can readily become if we are weak or immature in our response to them.

The Church has for too long paid little attention to most of the spiritual problems of the priest and particularly the two problems of contemplation and poverty. We were content with the clichés of the past long after they had lost all utility and relevance. Our present confusion is the price we must pay for our intellectual and spiritual flabbiness in face of the religious problems of the modern world. Please, God, let not the next generation of clergy have to pay the same price.

12

The Priest
in the Modern World

SEVERAL YEARS AGO I wandered into a hotel where the American Sociological Association was meeting, and was led off to a party by a colleague of mine. Everyone at the party save myself and the Assistant Secretary of Labor (whose Irish jaw dropped half a foot when he saw me enter the room) had gone to Townsend Harris High School in New York, City College of New York, and Columbia University. They had all been members of the Young Peoples' Socialist League, and had gone on to membership in the Trotskyite faction of the Communist party. They had all fought in the Second World War, and all were now distinguished full professors of sociology. As one of them said to me, "We began as Leninists, then we became Trotskyites, then socialists and social democrats, then supporters of the labor movement, then democrats, and finally sociologists."

These were some of the greats of the sociological profession and each in his own way had written about the basic experience of his life, an experience which one man summed up in the title of a book, *The End of Ideology.* Apparently each year at the sociology meetings they gather together to lament the dear dead days when they had a faith, a vision of the world to be remade, and an ideology which told them how to remake it. As one of them said to me, "We used to have something to believe in; we don't anymore but there is not one of us here who would not like to have an ideology once again."

The modern world is a place which both rejects faith and desperately looks for it. The priest of the modern world must, therefore, be perennially a man of faith, a man whose faith is so strong that he can dialogue about it with security and without the need to turn his dialogue into argument, a man who neither runs from controversies about religion nor imposes religious conversation on his friends, a man whose faith shines forth so completely in the sort of person he is and the kind of life he lives that he hardly needs to defend his position in words.

We have recently been told by some of the so-called radical theologians that God is dead (such an astonishing public relations gimmick for almost unintelligible theologizing is an interesting comment on our times). God is,

of course, not dead. If it were possible to kill him, I suspect he would have been more readily done to death by
the deadly academicisms of Catholic books about him
than he would by all the attacks of the radical theologians.
Apparently nominalism did not die with William of
Occam. The test is not whether God is dead but whether
he is relevant, and here the answer can only be, "You bet
your life he's relevant." At least he is if we give him a
chance, if we let him out of the absolutist categories and
the silly forms in which we have tried to imprison him.
The Lord has been relegated to dry theological manuals,
sterile debates, pious superstitions, and grotesque and
anachronistic churches. It is small wonder, insofar as we
permit him to manifest himself in such institutions, that
the modern world wonders if he is at all relevant. God,
of course, will tolerate our stupidities for just so long, and
will eventually break out from the prisons in which we
have tried to place him, and emerge from the tomb in
which our own superficial piety and academic theologizing has attempted to bury him. The modern world needs
him, and the third day is at hand.

The modern world seeks life, seeks resurrection. Brian
Wicker points this out with great insight:

By showing that this meeting of nature and grace has already
taken place, in the life, death and resurrection of Christ,
Christianity is able to offer an intelligible, even if incredible,

perspective in which the humanist moral vision can be freed
from its own intolerable paradox. The fact that to most people
the Christian perspective is incredible is relatively unimportant. For the first thing that is demanded is a perspective
which is relevant. Only if Christianity first appears to offer a
concept which is meaningful, can the possibility of its being
true be raised. . . . the relevance of the Christian concept of
death is that in it, death becomes something I enact, as a person who is in control. It is not consigning the body which I am
to oblivion, but consigning it to the possibility of its own completion from beyond itself. That this completion (or "glorifica-
tion") seems incredible to the humanist is due not only to
limited moral vision but to his entanglement with a secularist
philosophy that cannot fully support it. He cannot fully trust
his own instinct. The Christian is simply a humanist who has
learnt to trust the ground upon which he stands.*

The crazy thing is that the modern world seeks life
and resurrection. We have life and resurrection. We have
the risen Savior in our midst; only we do not really act
like we believe it, and if we do not act like we believe it,
how in the world can we expect the modern world to
believe it either?

We seem to be so little conscious of the fact of the
Savior's resurrection and his presence in the Church that
we almost overlook it as a basic difference between us
and those who are not of the house of the faith. If we

* *Toward A Contemporary Christianity*, 258–259.

had enough faith, then our hope and our joy and our love would be so powerful as to be irresistible. We are busy about many things—schools, organizations, projects, plans, and dreams. All of these are good, excellent, fine, wonderful, but they are not good enough without faith, and the critical question we must ask ourselves is whether we have faith.

Our response is quick: surely we have faith, aren't we priests? If we did not have faith, would we be priests? The question, however, is not one of whether we believe in God or not. The question is whether our faith is really a dynamic and contagious faith or whether it is not instead a timid, anxious, nervous, defensive, clogged, narrow faith—a faith which imprisons rather than liberates, a faith which takes away our courage rather than enhances it, a faith which stunts our humanity rather than stimulates it to further growth, a faith which causes us to lose ourselves in inertia, trivia, legalism, and self-serving defense mechanisms rather than a faith which can move mountains of apathy and indifference. Is it a faith which leads us to harass and disturb the People of God instead of encouraging and reassuring? The faith which gives life is the only kind of faith that is really worthy of the name. It is far more than just verbal assent to a series of propositions lifted out of the theology manuals or Denziger's Conciliar documents. Faith is not merely verbal nor merely passive. Faith cannot be construed as simply not having any doubts or difficulties. Faith is rather a driving, compelling, irresistible force which carries us through our life even into our death and then beyond.

All the other questions which we have discussed in these chapters ultimately become questions of faith. Unless we believe and believe powerfully, we will not be able to overcome our immaturity. We will not be able to grow in hope and love and in vision. We will not be able to preach the word of God, to build up the Christian community, to preside in charity over our people, to maintain high professional standards, to contemplate, to practice poverty, chastity, and obedience, to serve as members of the priestly collegium meshing our talents and abilities with the talents and abilities of others. All of these activities require faith and we can well imagine the Lord saying, "Father, do you really believe? Then, why don't you act like it?"

The priest of the modern world must, therefore, be above all else a man of faith, and it will take faith for him to read the signs of the times. It will take faith to give him the steadfastness, the nerve, the courage to ride the rapids of present ambiguity and confusion. It is only with faith that he will be able to achieve maturity. With faith, however, there seems to be no reason to doubt that ours is not only a critical time but a time of glorious opportunity, a time in which they who are *ex officio* the leaders of the People of God can lead the people to dramatic progress in preparing the way for the Lord's return.

We who are priests in the United States are fated neither to failure nor success in the present moment. We can begin a new golden age of Catholicism in this country if we have the courage, the vision, the wisdom, the maturity to be true to that which is best in our own American tradition, and the openness to put aside the irrelevant forms of the past in search of the magnificent opportunities of the present. Or, we can refuse to take chances. We can refuse to adjust. We can refuse to change. We can be content with our own narrowness, simplism, defensiveness, and insecurity. We can continue exercising most of our time and energy with the trivial concerns of the past while the barbarians surround the walls and batter the gates just as they did at Augustine's diocese as he lay on his deathbed. The laity, or at least an important element of them, are waiting. The Vatican Council has provided us with the theory, at least in broad outline. The Holy Spirit is hovering above us. The concluding question we must ask ourselves is, What are we waiting for?